# modern mix

16 Sewing Projects that Combine Designer Prints & Solid Fabrics

7 Quilts + Pillows, Bags & More

Jessica Levitt

Text copyright © 2011 by Jessica Levitt

Photography and Artwork copyright © 2011 by C&T Publishing, Inc.

Publisher: Amy Marson

Creative Director: Gailen Runge

Acquisitions Editor: Susanne Woods

Editor: Cynthia Bix

Technical Editors: Nanette S. Zeller and Carolyn Aune

Copyeditor/Proofreader: Wordfirm Inc

Cover/Book Designer: Kristy Zacharias

Page Layout Artist: April Mostek

Production Coordinator: Jenny Leicester

Production Editors: Julia Cianci and S. Michele Fry

Illustrators: Jessica Levitt and Tim Manibusan

Photography by Christina Carty-Francis and Diane Pedersen of C&T Publishing, Inc., unless otherwise noted

Published by Stash Books, an imprint of C&T Publishing, Inc., P.O. Box 1456, Lafayette, CA 94549

Library of Congress Cataloging-in-Publication Data

Levitt, Jessica.

Modern mix : 16 sewing projects that combine designer prints & solid fabrics : 7 quilts + pillows, bags & more / Jessica Levitt.

p. cm.

ISBN 978-1-60705-249-4 (soft cover)

1. Sewing. I. Title.

TT705.L46 2011

646.2--dc22

2010054237

Printed in China

10 9 8 7 6 5 4 3 2 1

## Dedication

For my husband, Jon, who believes in me, even when I can't.

## Acknowledgments

First, I have to thank my family for all their loving support and patience. To my husband and kids for putting up with less "mommy time" and for helping me achieve all my dreams. And to my mom, for teaching me to sew and giving me wings to fly on my own.

Thank you to Susanne Woods for starting me on this journey. And to all the wonderful people at C&T Publishing who have been so helpful, especially my editors, Cynthia Bix and Nanette Zeller.

Thanks to Rebecca Cobb for toiling away in the background, and to lots of other family and friends who contributed in countless ways.

Finally, my sincere appreciation goes to the entire wonderful craft-blogging community. Your work and acceptance inspires (and intimidates) me daily.

# contents

# Introduction

The process of sewing and the medium of fabric are so different from any other art form I've tried. And, believe me, I've tried quite a few. If you're already an avid sewist, you probably know what I'm talking about: I think it's the tactile nature of fabric and the functional character of quilts, bags, and other sewn crafts. Even if you can't call yourself an artist yet (it took me a long, long time), you can sit in front of your machine and create. Anybody can. Really.

So, more than anything, what I hope for is for you to be fearless.

Sewing isn't that hard, but it's often intimidating. This book isn't a comprehensive guide to sewing or quilting, but if you've got some basic skills, you should be able to make any of the projects successfully. So don't be afraid. And if you're more than a little experienced, I invite you to step outside your comfort zone and try something you haven't before. That might mean a technique you've shied away from or even just choosing fabric and colors that aren't your norm.

What you'll end up with is art you can use. That's what I really love about sewing. Sure, there are artists who sew amazing art quilts to hang on a wall. They're fabulous, and their beauty alone is a function. But I think sewing something that you or some lucky recipient is going to use has an extra level of satisfaction. You can quite literally wrap yourself in the love that quiltmakers put into their work.

Which brings us to the medium: fabric. Oh, how I love fabric. The choices and combinations are endless. And the colors and patterns are so inspiring. I mean, here's a creative endeavor that allows you to choose someone else's art, cut it up, combine it, and make it your own. What could be better? My own personal stash is quite large and growing every day.

But in all my passion for the beautiful patterns of printed fabrics, I realized I was often forgetting about solids. And what a shame, because there are so many advantages to adding solid-colored fabrics to your work: First, it can focus more attention on the piecing, and that's all your hard work, right? Also, you can use solid fabrics to highlight some of your favorite prints. These stand out more when used in combination with solids. And solid fabrics are certainly less expensive, so if you're using large quantities, you can save a lot of money by adding some solids. Finally, there's a clean, modern look that you just can't get with printed fabric alone. And these are only a few of the advantages to using solid fabrics that quickly come to mind.

I challenged myself to come up with projects that used both designer prints we all love and luscious solid fabrics. The quantities of each vary from project to project, as does their purpose in the project. I've divided them in chapters based on the solids' function, but I do hope you'll be fearless and change it up as you see fit.

# materials and design basics

Making exciting
choices for
your projects

# Fabric

Unless otherwise noted, all the projects in this book use what is known as quilter's cotton. It's 100% cotton and widely available in fabric and quilt shops. It comes in a standard 42″–45″ width in a variety of prints and solids.

There are different levels of quality of this cotton, and I highly recommend you buy your fabric in a quilt shop, either online or brick-and-mortar, to ensure the highest level of quality. If you are going to put so much effort and love into a project, it's best to ensure that it will provide the results you're aiming for and will wear well over the years.

## SOLID FABRICS

Several manufacturers produce beautiful, colored cotton solids that are widely available. For this book I used exclusively Kona Cotton Solids by Robert Kaufman. These come in more than 200 colors and are fabulous to work with. I've listed the specific colors used in each project in Resources (page 127) for your reference. Some may become unavailable over time, but the most popular ones stick around for many years. If you can afford it, a nice stash of a wide range of solid-colored fabrics is great to have on hand. It allows you to audition colors with the prints you have chosen. You can also get a color card with swatches of all the Kona Solids on it, which will definitely make shopping online easier.

In a couple of projects I use linen as one of my solid fabrics. Linen or a linen blend fabric has a beautiful texture and simplicity to it. It comes in many shades of beige or tan, and even a variety of colors.

Finally, you might choose a pattern that calls for muslin, an inexpensive all-cotton fabric often used for making mock-ups of patterns before cutting into your actual yardage. It can be purchased in a variety of widths, but for the purpose of this book, I'll assume you will buy 36″–40″ wide.

You might consider using a flat sheet for the backing of your larger quilts. If you find one large enough, you won't have to piece it at all, and it may be less expensive. Just make sure to get high-quality cotton sheets.

## FABRIC PREPARATION

It's often a good idea to prewash your fabric before cutting. It helps prevent colors from running or fabrics from shrinking differently. When I prewash, I simply run like-colored fabrics through a warm rinse cycle in my machine and dry them in the dryer. Then, of course, you have to press them before cutting.

That said, I often skip this step. Fabrics are so well made today and the colors don't often run. Prewashing does add some extra time to a project, and usually I just can't wait to get going (I'm all about instant gratification). When I'm working with hand-dyed fabric or using a very light fabric with darks, or if absolutely no shrinkage is key to the project, I might take the time.

## fabric anatomy

Fabric most often comes folded in half on a cardboard bolt. The edges that are "finished" are called the selvages, and the edges that are cut to length are the cut edges. The grain of the fabric runs perpendicular to the selvages. The bias of fabric is on the diagonal.

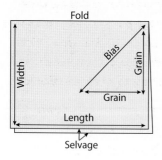

Fabric is bought in increments of ⅛ of a yard. Most pattern yardage in this book allows for fabric shrinkage and the cutting of an extra strip or an additional ⅛ yard in case of a goof.

## Other Essentials

### THREAD

Tons of different kinds of thread are on the market. Make sure you use the type of thread suited for your intended application and fabric, or you'll wind up with headaches. My favorite for quilting and the other projects in this book is high-quality 100% cotton thread. All-purpose polyester thread or even cotton-wrapped polyester thread will work just fine for piecing. Beautiful, shiny rayon thread is used for embroidery; you should not use it for piecing. For machine quilting, 100% cotton, polyester, and rayon threads are good choices.

### BATTING

Batting is the middle layer of a quilt that gives it body and warmth. The type of batting to use is a personal decision; you can consult your local quilt shop for guidance. Note that your batting choice will affect how much quilting is necessary for the quilt. Check the manufacturer's instructions to see how far apart the quilting lines can be.

I've experimented with several types of batting through the years, and I prefer the natural fibers of cotton batting. In several cases, I found that the fibers of polyester batting actually worked their way through the cotton fabric, and I was disappointed. I most often work with cotton batting from the Warm Company. It's called Warm & Natural (though some very light or white quilts call for Warm & White). Batting can be bought by the yard in several different widths, including 34″, 45″, 90″, and 124″, or in prepackaged sizes. In addition to choosing the fiber, you can also choose the loft, which is the thickness or fluffiness of a batting. Most quilters use thin batting. When determining batting size requirements, I allow for a 4″ overhang on each side of the quilt top.

## INTERFACING

Sometimes referred to as stabilizer, interfacing is used as an inner layer to create shape or stiffness. It comes in a variety of thicknesses, as well as sew-in or fusible versions and wovens or nonwovens.

Interfacing is made by several manufacturers. Each brand has its own labeling, which usually tells you what type of fabric it is for and/or how much stability it provides. Projects in this book mostly call for nonwoven, mid- to heavyweight sew-in interfacing. Examples of this are Pellon 40 and Pellon 50. For very stiff project needs, you can use an extra-heavy sewable interfacing that's as thick as thin cardboard. Brand names available are Timtex (available from C&T Publishing) or Peltex, but others are available also.

## FUSIBLE WEB

Fusible web is a material that can be ironed between two pieces of fabric that will permanently bond the fabrics together. Many varieties are available, some with paper on one or both sides and some without paper. The paper acts as a protective covering so that the adhesive doesn't melt to your iron. Fusibles without the paper backing require a Teflon pressing sheet, freezer paper, or release paper (available from C&T Publishing). The basic process is to iron the fusible onto the wrong side of one fabric, remove the paper backing or protective covering, and iron the fusible-backed fabric onto another fabric.

The fusible web I most often use is called Steam-a-Seam 2 and has a paper backing on both sides. It also has a temporary (repositionable) adhesive on both sides.

With this type of double-sided, paper-backed fusible, you can draw your design onto the paper side of the backing (in reverse), trim loosely around the edges, peel off the other paper layer, and stick it onto the fabric. The temporary adhesive will hold it in place as you cut along the lines through the paper backing and the fabric at the same time, peel off the remaining paper, and stick it on your background fabric. When you're satisfied with the placement, iron for a permanent bond.

## NOTIONS

Some projects in this book call for notions such as buttons, other closures, zippers, or grommets. These items will be described in the project materials lists and should be widely available in your local fabric shops.

## Design and Color

Even when you are using a pattern from a book, there is still design work involved in sewing: most notably, the choice and placement of fabrics and colors.

Your first option is to mimic what I've used in the projects. Because Kona Cotton colors are often readily available, I've listed the colors of the solids I used in Resources (page 127). The same prints may prove more difficult to get your hands on, but you can do your best to create a similar look.

However, I recommend you try it your own way. Be fearless, remember? If my quilt is pink, orange, and brown, you might change it to green, blue, and brown.

And when you do make changes, you should take certain design "rules" into consideration. For each fabric you choose, consider three criteria: *hue, value,* and *scale.* And for how they all work together, think about levels of *contrast.*

**HUE** is the color or colors in a fabric. If you aren't already familiar with the color wheel, here is a simple example. You can search the Internet for many more elaborate ones or buy a tool such as the 3-in-1 Color Tool from C&T Publishing.

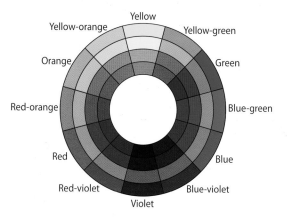

Different colors reflect different moods. Red, orange, and yellow are warm colors, while green, blue, and purple are cool colors. How do certain colors make you feel?

**VALUE** is the lightness or darkness of a fabric. If you're trying to compare two fabrics to determine which is darker, a tool like a green or red value finder (included in the 3-in-1 Color Tool) is useful. Or you can try squinting your eyes until you don't really see the colors anymore—just the darkness or lightness.

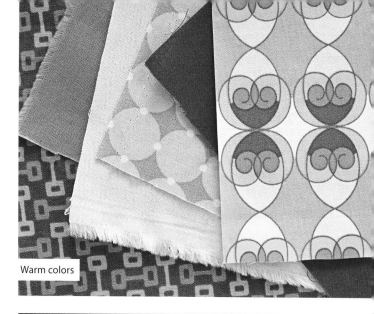

Warm colors

Cool colors

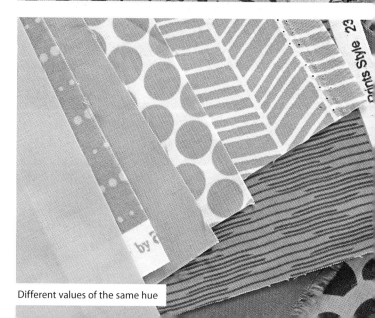

Different values of the same hue

**SCALE** is the size of the print on a fabric—small, medium, or large scale. Contrast also plays a part here. For example, you could have very large print made up of two colors that are very close to one another on the color wheel (see page 10), and your eye would read it as almost a solid. Consider the scale and definition of a print when you look at the size of the pieces you will use and how they are placed next to one another. A simple, small patchwork of a large-scale, high-definition print might feel too busy for some, but others love the look. It's your call.

Small-, medium-, and large-scale prints of the same hue and value

**CONTRAST** is how the hues, values, and scale all work in relation to one another. Black and white solids would be very high contrast. Looking back at the color wheel, you'll notice that colors opposite from one another (called *complementary* colors), like blue and orange, have high contrast; and those next to each other (called *analogous* colors), such as red and orange, have very little contrast. So if you wanted to create a lot of contrast, you might choose a light yellow and a dark purple, but if you wanted minimal contrast, you'd choose a medium red and a medium red-orange.

How much contrast you want in each situation is a personal preference. In general, if you

use less contrast, your quilts and projects will appear soft (or even "flat"), and the pattern of the piecing will be subtle and less noticeable. But if you use high-contrast fabrics, the sewn pattern or design will stand out much more. I would say that most projects call for a bit of both!

In many of my projects, I like to use analogous colors. But by adding some variety in the value and hue, they have a depth to them. I also make sure to provide some strong contrast to create the pattern.

In *Twin String* Quilt (page 63) I used a variety of values of magenta and fuchsia, with strong contrasting solids.

If you like what I've done in a project but you want to change the fabrics and colors, take a moment to notice how I've used contrast, and try to duplicate that.

# Back Me Up

Using solid fabrics as a background for your favorite prints

## Materials

**15–25 various bright prints:** 1 fat quarter or ¼ yard each; a minimum of 4½ yards total (for circles)

**Solid 1:** 2⅞ yards (for accent strip)

**Solid 2:** 7 yards (for main quilt top)

**Backing:** 9 yards

**Binding:** ¾ yard for straight-grain binding (1 yard for bias binding)

**Batting:** 3 yards of 124″ wide (or packaged king size)

**8–10 various circular objects** (paper plates, cans, tins, cardboard cake rounds, ribbon spools), in sizes ranging from 3″ to 11″, to use as circle templates

**Permanent marker**

**Erasable fabric marker or chalk**

## Cutting

### FROM SOLID 1:

Trim one selvage edge; then cut 1 strip 22″ × 97″ from the length of fabric [A]

### FROM SOLID 2:

*Refer to the cutting diagram (page 16). All pieces are cut with the longer dimension going across the width of the fabric.*

Cut 3 rectangles 41½″ × 33″ [B]

Cut 3 rectangles 33″ × 23″ [C]

Cut 2 rectangles 41½″ × 29½″ [D]

Cut 1 rectangle 29½″ × 16″ [E]

# pebble road quilt

**FINISHED SIZE:** 112½″ × 97″

The bright floral "pebbles" against a background of solid gray give this king-size quilt a real *wow!* factor. The appliquéd circles are created with a finished edge for simplicity and ease of handling. They're a lot of fun to play with; arrange the colors and patterns until your composition feels just right. If you've been intimidated by the idea of sewing a whole bed-sized quilt, this may be just the project for your modern bedroom.

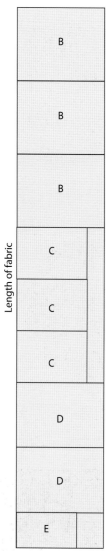

B

B

B

C

C

C

D

D

E

Length of fabric

Width of fabric

Cutting diagram

Make more of the smaller circles than of the larger ones; the smaller ones are easier to place.

# Construction

*All seams are ½˝ unless otherwise noted.*

## Make the circle appliqués

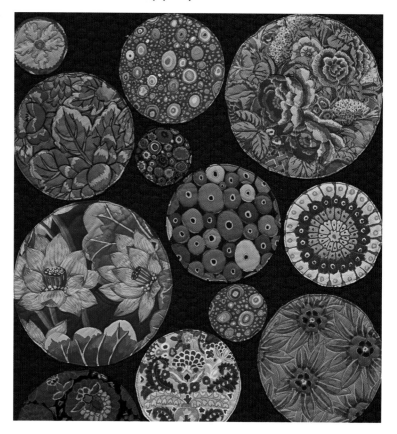

### CUT OUT THE CIRCLES

You will need approximately 60 circles. Obviously the final number will depend on the size of your circles and even the size of your quilt.

**1.** Use the circular objects as templates and trace several circles of different sizes onto the wrong side of each bright print fabric with a permanent marker. Make sure to leave approximately ¾˝ to 1˝ between any 2 circles. Fussy cut the circles, if desired, by placing the circles based on the design of the fabric. In many instances I chose to center a flower or motif in my circle.

**2.** Cut out the circles loosely, leaving about ½˝ outside the traced line. There is no need to do this perfectly; they will be trimmed later.

## SEW THE CIRCLES

**1.** Pin the circles right side *down* on the leftover Solid 1 fabric. Save fabric by placing them as closely as possible without overlapping. Pin frequently (about every 1″ to 2″) around the edges so they lie nice and flat (Figure 1).

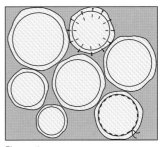

Figure 1

Pin a lot of the circles at once. For ease of sewing, cut up the solid fabric into "chunks" of about 2 or 3 circles (more or fewer, depending on your preference). Just loosely cut the solid fabric around the circles for now.

**2.** Sew just inside the traced line on each circle (Figure 1). Make sure the stitches are inside the line or else the marker line will show on the finished circle. Sew completely around each circle.

**3.** Trim the circles, cutting neatly through both layers of fabric and leaving approximately a ¼″ seam allowance all the way around.

**4.** Notch the curved seam allowance all the way around, being careful not to snip the seam. For a smooth curve, notch about every ¼″, evenly spaced. Flip the circle, solid fabric facing up, and with very sharp scissors, snip a slit about 2″ to 3″ long in the center of the solid fabric only (Figure 2). Be very careful not to cut the print fabric at all!

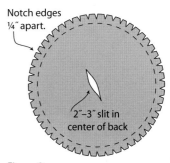

Notch edges ¼″ apart.

2″–3″ slit in center of back

Figure 2

**5.** Turn the circle right side out through the slit. Use your finger or an eraser end of a pencil to make sure the edges are pushed all the way out so it has a perfect circle shape. Press flat.

## Make the quilt top

**1.** Mark the seam allowance on the 22″ × 97″ accent strip of Solid 1 fabric [A], using an erasable fabric marker or chalk. Mark a line ½″ in from each of the two long edges; then mark a line 1″ in from each of the short edges.

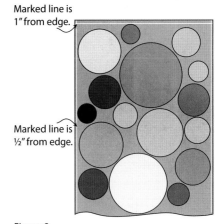

Marked line is 1″ from edge.

Marked line is ½″ from edge.

Figure 3

**2.** Lay the strip flat on the floor and place the circles all over it, print side up. Position the circles right up to the marked lines, but not over them. Try to vary the sizes, fitting them closely together (leaving about a ¼″ space between the closest ones), and filling up the most possible space. Since the circles have a nice finished edge, there's no problem rearranging them until you like how it looks (Figure 3).

## NOTE

At this point, you may need to go back and make a few more circles of a particular size to fill a gap, or you might have some left over.

**3.** Pin the circles in place once they have been placed as desired. (If you prefer not to work with so many pins, hand baste each circle with a contrasting thread to be removed later.)

**4.** Topstitch each circle in place ⅛˝ from the edge.

**5.** Refer to the quilt assembly diagram (below) to piece the quilt top using ½˝ seams. Trim the outer edges even, and square up the quilt top.

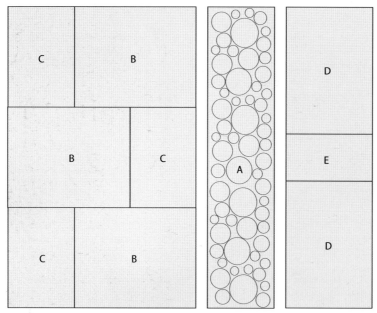

Quilt assembly diagram

**6.** Refer to Quiltmaking Basics on pages 119–124 for directions on how to layer, baste, quilt, and bind your quilt.

*Admire your stunning new quilt!*

## Materials

**Linen/linen blend:** ¾ yard (for apron skirt)

**Solid fabric:** ¾ yard (for waistband, facing, and ties)

**Print scraps:** at least 8 different prints
 (for appliquéd strips and waistband)*

**Medium-weight interfacing:** ⅛ yard

**Erasable fabric marker or chalk**

*See sizes under Cutting.*

### tip

You can use a 20″ × 30″ tea towel instead of linen for the skirt of the apron. Just cut off 1½″ from the top edge, and your other edges will already be finished for you! You'll have to wrap the appliqué strips around to the back and hem them separately.

## Cutting

### FROM THE LINEN:

Cut 1 rectangle 31″ × 20½″

### FROM THE SOLID:

Cut 1 strip 3″ × width of fabric; crosscut into

 4 rectangles 1¾″ × 3″

 3 rectangles 2″ × 3″

 3 rectangles 2¼″ × 3″

 4 rectangles 2½″ × 3″

 3 rectangles 2¾″ × 3″

Cut 1 strip 4¼″ × width of fabric; crosscut into
1 rectangle 4¼″ × 22″ (for waistband facing)

Cut 2 strips 5½ × width of fabric (for ties)

*Cutting continued on page 22*

# linen apron

**FINISHED SIZE:** 30″ long × 21″ wide plus ties

Designed for everyday wear, this linen apron does its job in style. Brighten up a very simple base with some of your favorite print scraps. By keeping the solid fabrics in neutral colors and adding a variety of prints, you'll end up with an apron that matches almost anything you wear.

## FROM VARIOUS PRINT SCRAPS:

Cut 1 strip 2½″ × 10½″ [A]

Cut 1 strip 2¼″ × 9½″ [B]

Cut 1 strip 2¼″ × 12″ [C]

Cut 1 strip 2¾″ × 8″ [D]

Cut 1 strip 1¾″ × 9½″ [E]

Cut 1 strip 2½″ × 10¾″ [F]

Cut 1 strip 2″ × 8¾″ [G]

Cut 1 strip 2¼″ × 9½″ [H]

Cut 4 rectangles 1¾″ × 3½″

Cut 3 rectangles 2″ × 3½″

Cut 3 rectangles 2¼″ × 3½″

Cut 4 rectangles 2½″ × 3½″

Cut 3 rectangles 2¾″ × 3½″

From the interfacing:

Cut 1 rectangle 4″ × 22″

# Construction

*All seams are ½″ unless otherwise noted.*

## Sew the apron skirt

**1.** Hem (page 119) the sides of the linen rectangle by pressing under ½″ on the short (21″) sides. Tuck the raw edges into the fold and press again. Topstitch ⅛″ from the folded edge. (Skip this step if using a tea towel, see Tip, page 21.)

**2.** Sew strips A–H together in order as shown in Figure 1, lining up the bottom short edges and leaving the top edges staggered. On each seam, stop sewing ½″ from the top of the shorter strip (to allow for turning under). Backstitch at both ends. Press the seam allowances open. Press all the raw edges, except for the bottom, under ½″

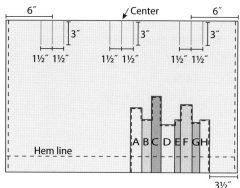

Figure 1

**3.** Position the pieced print strip on the front of the linen rectangle 3½″ from the right edge and aligning the bottom raw edges (Figure 1). Pin in place. (If using a tea towel, see Tip, page 21.)

**4.** Topstitch close to all the edges to hold it in place.

**5.** Press the bottom raw edge of the rectangle under ¼″ and again 1¾″ from that. Pin in place and stitch close to the pressed edge to complete the hem.

**6.** Mark the center of the top raw edge, and mark 1½″ on either side of the center. Also mark 6″ from each top corner and 1½″ on either side of these marks (Figure 1).

**7.** Draw a 3″ line down from the raw edge at each mark, using chalk or an erasable marker.

Always check your marking method on a scrap of the material you are using to be sure it doesn't leave a permanent mark. You've probably heard that before, but who wants their hard work ruined because they forgot to test a marker?

**8.** Fold the two adjacent lines in to meet the center line. Press and pin in place. Topstitch ⅛″ from the center top edge down to the 3″ line. Turn the fabric 90° and sew several stitches to the other side of center. Backstitch over those stitches several times. Turn the fabric 90° again and continue to sew ⅛″ along the other side of the center, returning to the top edge (Figure 2).

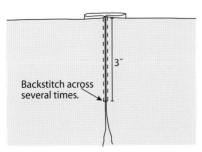

Backstitch across several times.

3″

Figure 2

**9.** Repeat Step 8 for the other 2 sets of marked lines to form the 3 pleats.

## Prepare the waistband

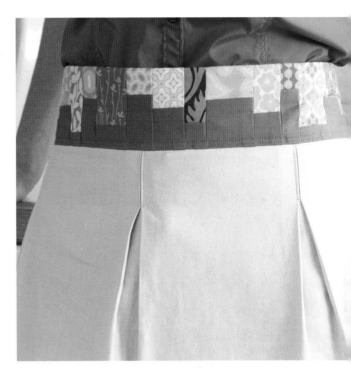

**1.** Pair each small print rectangle with a solid rectangle of the same width. With right sides together, sew across the width with a ½″ seam. Press the seam allowance toward the solid fabric. Each sewn pair should measure 5½″ long.

**2.** Lay out all the pairs in a row with the print side at the top and the top edges touching the same line on your cutting mat. Arrange in a pleasing manner so the colors and widths are varied (Figure 3).

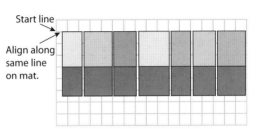

Start line

Align along same line on mat.

Figure 3

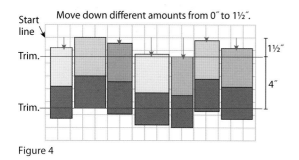

Start line

Move down different amounts from 0″ to 1½″.

Trim.

1½″

4″

Trim.

Figure 4

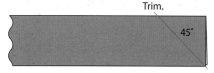

Trim.

45°

Figure 5

Trim corners.

Figure 6

**3.** Stagger the pairs by leaving some where they are and moving others up to 1½″ down. Being careful to keep the pairs straight and in place, use your ruler and rotary cutter to trim all the strips along the top print side 1½″ from the line they were originally lined up on. The ones you moved down 1½″ won't be trimmed at all. Now trim each pair along the solid fabric to a total length of 4″ (Figure 4).

**4.** Sew the pairs together along the 4″ sides, right sides together and using a ½″ seam, to create one long strip. Sew the pairs in the same order as they are laid out. Press the seam allowances to one side.

**5.** Position the 4″ × 22″ interfacing to the wrong side of the pieced strip. Pin frequently; then baste around the edges with a ¼″ seam.

**6.** Pin the 4¼″ × 22″ solid waistband facing, right sides together, to the top print fabric edge of the pieced strip. Sew across this edge with a ½″ seam.

**7.** Press under ½″ along the long raw edge of the attached facing. Fold and press the waistband facing behind the pieced strip, wrong sides together.

## Make the ties

**1.** Fold each tie in half lengthwise, right sides together, and pin raw edges together. Cut off a 45° triangle across 1 short end of each tie (Figure 5).

**2.** Sew across the angled end and along the long edges with a ½″ seam (Figure 6). Trim the corners at an angle and turn right side out. Press flat.

# Finish the apron

**1.** Open the pressed waistband and center the long raw edge of the pieced strip to the top of the apron skirt as shown in Figure 7. The waistband will extend ½˝ on each side of the skirt. Pin and sew using a ½˝ seam. Press toward the waistband.

**2.** Position the ties on the right side of the pieced waistband strip (Figure 8). On each side of the waistband, align the raw edges and line up the top edge of the tie with the facing seam. Pin and baste with a ¼˝ seam.

**3.** Press the short sides of the waistband (and the ties) under ½˝ (Figure 9).

**4.** Fold the waistband facing to the back of the pieced strip, wrong sides together. Pin along the skirt edge, catching all layers and making sure the bottom edge of the facing stays folded under and covers the seam. Also pin the sides, making sure the raw edges stay folded in ½˝ and the tie ends are free (Figure 10).

**5.** Topstitch close to the top and bottom edges of the waistband and topstitch again ⅛˝ in from that stitching. Topstitch close to the edge along the folded-under sides of the waistband; then reverse over the stitching and back again to secure the ties (Figure 10).

*Now you're ready to cook in style.*

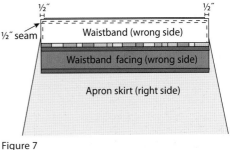

Figure 7

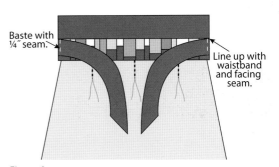

Figure 8

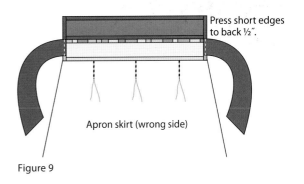

Figure 9

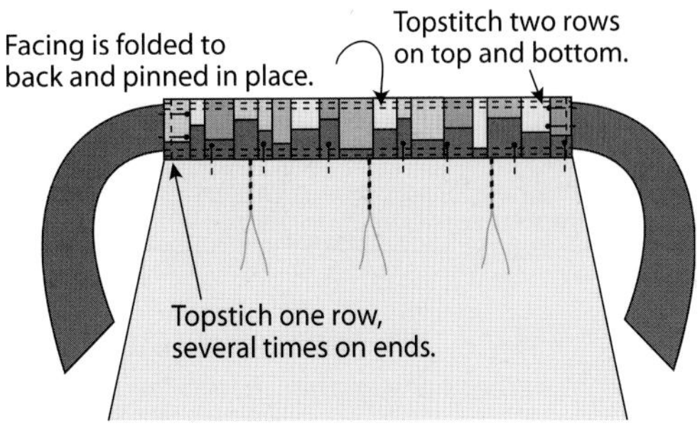

Figure 10

## Materials

**Pink Prints 1, 2, and 3:**
1 fat quarter each (for blocks)

**Orange Prints 1, 2, and 3:**
1 fat quarter each (for blocks)

**Brown Prints 1, 2, and 3:**
1 fat quarter each (for blocks)

**Orange Print 4:** ⅝ yard (for Border 2)

**White Solid:** 7 yards (for background and Borders 1 and 3)

**Binding:** ¾ yard for straight-grain binding (⅞ yard for bias binding)

**Backing:** 8⅞ yards

**Batting:** 3 yards of 124″ wide (or packaged king size)

## tip

When choosing your fabrics, try to pick prints that contain colors in common with each other. For example, if your quilt is orange, pink, and brown, then choose a pink fabric with some brown or orange in it. This helps to unify your quilt's color palette.

# frame up quilt

**FINISHED BLOCK:** 19″ × 19″
**FINISHED QUILT:** 95½″ × 95½″

There's no cleaner way to highlight some of your favorite prints than to use a whole lot of white as the background. This modern quilt is a generous queen size, and using mostly solid fabrics makes it much more affordable. It has two block variations, but their large size and the fact that both centers are the same make this an achievable quilt, even for beginners. And there's lots of potential for playing with the colors here—imagine a dark background…

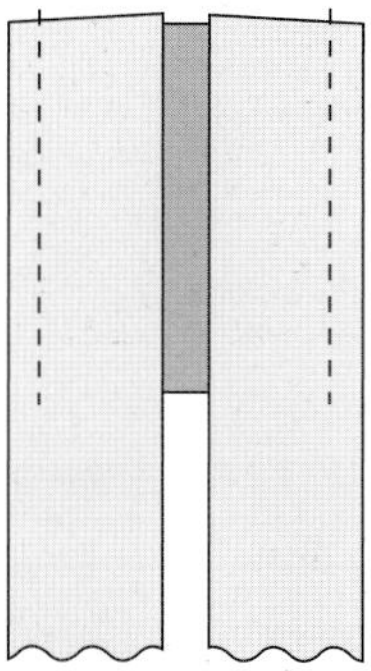

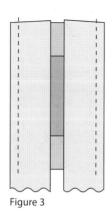

Figure 1

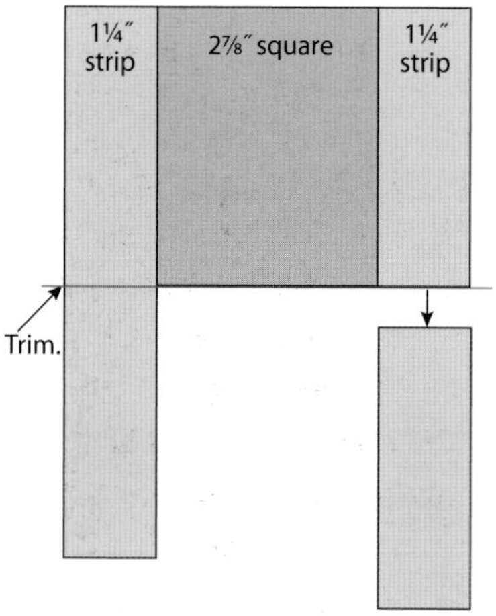

1¼″ strip | 2⅞″ square | 1¼″ strip

Trim.

Figure 2

Figure 3

# Cutting

**FROM EACH FAT QUARTER:**

Cut 4 strips 2″ × 18″

Cut 7 strips 1¼″ × 18″

Cut 2 squares 2⅞″ × 2⅞″

Cut the remaining fabric into 1¼″ strips for piecing the B Block borders

**FROM ORANGE PRINT 4:**

Cut 9 strips 2″ × width of fabric (for Border 2)

**FROM WHITE SOLID:**

Cut 12 strips 6⅝″ × width of fabric

Cut 12 strips 5⅞″ × width of fabric

From the remaining fabric trim one selvage edge; then

Cut 4 strips 2½″ × *length of fabric* (for Border 1)

Cut 4 strips 6½″ × *length of fabric* (for Border 3)

# Construction

*All seams are a scant ¼″ unless otherwise noted.*

There are two different blocks in this quilt. Both have the same center framed by white, but Block B has an outer border pieced from the print fabrics.

## Sew the block centers

Sew all the block centers using the quilt assembly diagram (page 30) as your guide for fabric placement. Or, assemble the block centers in your own pleasing combination.

**1.** Sew a 1¼″ strip onto 2 opposite sides of a 2⅞″ square, right sides together (Figure 1). Do not cut the strips down to length before sewing. Press the seam allowance toward the strips. Now, use your ruler and rotary cutter to trim the strips even with the edges of the square (Figure 2). Next, sew a strip onto the remaining

2 sides (Figure 3). Again press toward the strips. Then trim these strips off even with the edges of the first strips to create a square that should be approximately 4⅜″ × 4⅜″. Repeat this entire step to make 16 centers, saving the leftover strips for the B Block borders.

> Because you will be trimming down the final blocks, it is not imperative that your seams be exactly a scant ¼″. But it's best to be consistent.

**2.** Repeat Step 1 using the 2″ strips around the 4⅜″ pieced centers. The finished block centers should be approximately 7⅜″ × 7⅜″.

**3.** Refer to the quilt assembly diagram (page 30) to determine which block centers are for the A Blocks and which are for the B Blocks. Separate the block centers into 8 A Blocks and 8 B Blocks.

## Complete the A Blocks

**1.** Add the 6⅝″ white, solid strips to the 8 A Block centers. Do this in the same manner as in Sew the Block Centers, Step 1.

**2.** Trim the completed A Blocks to measure 19½″ × 19½″. Trim equal amounts from all 4 sides so they don't wind up lopsided.

## Complete the B Blocks

**1.** Add the 5⅞″ white strips to the 8 B Block centers. Do this in the same manner as in Sew the Block Centers, Step 1.

**2.** Trim the completed B Blocks to measure 18″ × 18″. Again, carefully trim equal amounts from all 4 sides so they don't wind up lopsided.

**3.** Piece random lengths of the remaining 1¼″ strips together for the B Block border. Either cut the strips into varying lengths (from 1″ to 10″) and then sew them together end-to-end, or snip them off at random lengths as they are sewn together. Make 6 strips, each a little over 100″ in length. Make more if needed. Press the seams in one direction.

**4.** Add the pieced strips to the 18″ × 18″ B Blocks in the same manner as previous steps. Here, it is important to have an accurate ¼″ seam allowance to end up with a final block size of 19½″ × 19½″.

# Complete the quilt

**1.** Refer to the quilt assembly diagram below and sew the 4 rows of 4 blocks together. Press all the seams toward the B Blocks, including the long seams that join the rows (which means switching the pressing direction at each square).

> When assembling a quilt, you may want to number the blocks to keep track of them as you sew. Pin the numbers on each block and you'll always know where they belong.

**2.** Refer to Quiltmaking Basics (pages 119–120) for how to sew on borders. Press the seam allowances toward the colored fabric.

**3.** Refer to Quiltmaking Basics (pages 119–124) for directions on how to layer, baste, quilt, and bind your quilt.

*Now spread it out for a beautiful bed. Perhaps some new pillowcases are in order?*

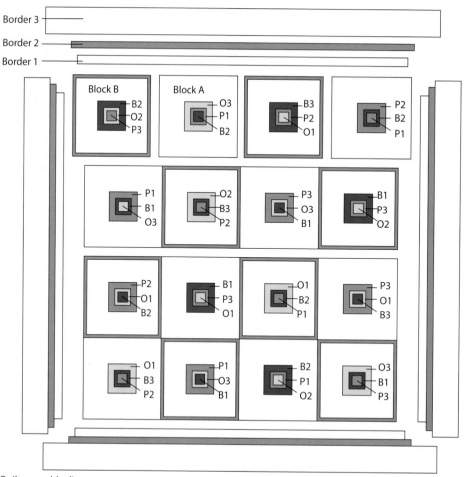

Quilt assembly diagram

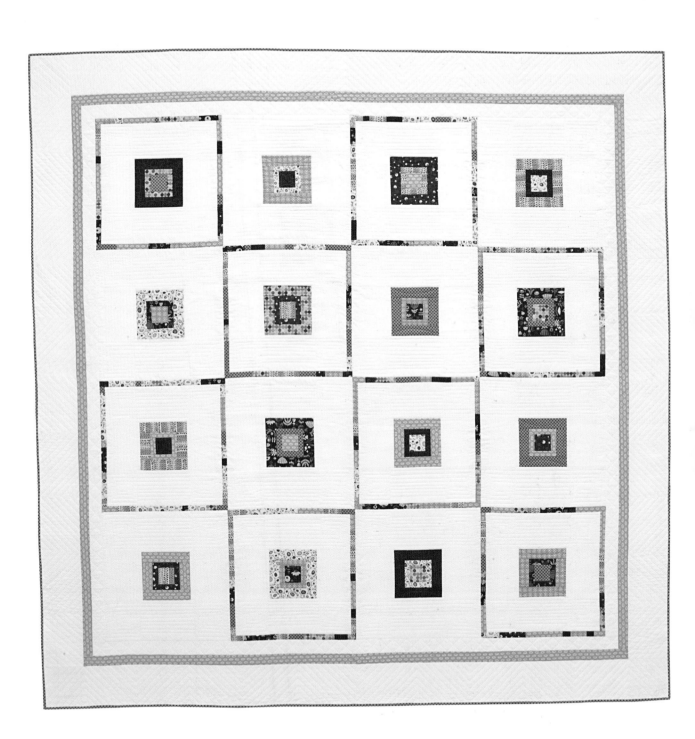

The directions are for three popular sizes, but the length is easily altered to fit your table. You could even make only the center if you just want a table runner.

## Materials

To choose a size, measure your table top. You should allow for an overhang of 8″ to 15″ on each side. So to calculate your tablecloth size, double the amount of overhang (16″ to 30″) and add this to each dimension of your table top.

No matter what size you choose, you will need 6 different fabrics:

**Prints 1 and 2** for center squares

**Print 3** for center background*

**Print 4** for outer stripes

**Solid 1** for inner stripes

**Solid 2** for main body

*A solid fabric would work equally well in place of the Print 3 fabric.*

### NOTE
In this particular project, prewashing your fabrics is important. You want the cloth to lie flat, and you will most likely be washing it frequently after use.

# color block tablecloth

**FINISHED CLOTH, SIZE 1:** 54″ × 74″

**FINISHED CLOTH, SIZE 2:** 72″ × 108″

**FINISHED CLOTH, SIZE 3:** 72″ × 126″

If you already have too many quilts at home or you want to fancy up your dining room, this might be the project for you. Essentially it's a quilt top that you never put the back on. The design is simple to keep the seams to a minimum, so that it wears well even with lots of washings. The design is also great for showing off your favorite large-scale fabrics.

## Size 1 (54″ × 74″)

| FABRIC | YARDAGE | CUTTING |
|---|---|---|
| Print 1 | ⅜ yard or 1 fat quarter | 3 squares 9″ × 9″ |
| Print 2 | ⅜ yard or 1 fat quarter | 2 squares 9″ × 9″ |
| Print 3 | ¾ yard | 3 strips 4½″ × width of fabric; crosscut 1 in half<br>4 rectangles 3¼″ × 9″ [A]<br>2 rectangles 3½″ × 9″ [B] |
| Print 4 | ⅝ yard | 3 strips 5″ × width of fabric; crosscut 1 in half |
| Solid 1 | ⅜ yard | 3 strips 2½″ × width of fabric; crosscut 1 in half |
| Solid 2 | 3¼ yards | 2 rectangles 25″ × 55″* |

*You can easily adjust the length of the tablecloth by changing the 25″ width of these rectangles to any measurement up to the width of your fabric.*

## Size 2 (72″ × 108″)

| FABRIC | YARDAGE | CUTTING |
|---|---|---|
| Print 1 | ⅜ yard | 3 squares 11″ × 11″ |
| Print 2 | ⅜ yard | 2 squares 11″ × 11″ |
| Print 3 | 1 yard | 4 strips 5″ × width of fabric<br>4 rectangles 4½″ × 11″ [A]<br>2 rectangles 5″ × 11″ [B] |
| Print 4 | ⅞ yard | 4 strips 6″ × width of fabric |
| Solid 1 | ½ yard | 4 strips 3″ × width of fabric |
| Solid 2 | 4¼ yards | 2 rectangles 39″ × 73″* |

*You can easily adjust the length of the tablecloth by changing the 39″ width of these rectangles to any measurement up to the width of your fabric.*

## Size 3 (72″ × 126″)

| FABRIC | YARDAGE | CUTTING |
|---|---|---|
| Print 1 | ⅜ yard | 3 squares 12″ × 12″ |
| Print 2 | ⅜ yard | 2 squares 12″ × 12″ |
| Print 3 | 1½ yards | 4 strips 9½″ × width of fabric<br>4 rectangles 4″ × 12″ [A]<br>2 rectangles 3½″ × 12″ [B] |
| Print 4 | 1 yard | 4 strips 7″ × width of fabric |
| Solid 1 | ½ yard | 4 strips 3½″ × width of fabric |
| Solid 2 | 4¼ yards | 2 rectangles 41½″ × 73″* |

*You can easily adjust the length of the tablecloth by changing the 41½″ width of these rectangles to any measurement up to the width of your fabric.*

# Construction

*All seams are ½″ unless otherwise noted.*

As you sew each seam, also finish the raw edges of the seam allowance. Some sewing machines have special stitches to do this, but it can be done by zigzagging over the raw edges after you've sewn the seams. Or, you can finish the seams with a serger, if you have one. Do this for every seam because the tablecloth will not have a backing.

## Sew the center column

**1.** Refer to the assembly diagram (page 35) to arrange and sew the Print 1 and Print 2 squares to the Print 3 [A and B] rectangles, using a ½″ seam allowance. Press the seam allowances toward Print 3.

### tip

When I sew the pieces together, I use a thread color that matches Print 3. And, if you don't want your topstitching to show, match the color of your topstitching thread to the various fabrics in the tablecloth.

**2.** Topstitch ⅛″ from the seam on top of all the seam allowances (Print 3 side) to hold them flat and in place.

**3.** Trim the selvage ends from 2 strips of Print 3 (for Size 1, use 1 full strip and 1 half strip). Sew the strips together end-to-end. Press the seam allowances to one side and topstitch ⅛″ from the seam on top of the seam allowance. Repeat this step with the remaining strips.

You can piece the strips together diagonally as you would binding or borders (see Quiltmaking Basics, pages 119-124). You will have just enough fabric, and this will make the seams less noticeable.

**4.** Cut the 2 long Print 3 strips to length: 55″ for Size 1, or 73″ for Sizes 2 and 3.

**5.** Sew a long strip to each side of the center as shown in the assembly diagram at right. Press the seams toward the long strips and topstitch ⅛″ from the seam on top of the seam allowance.

# Add the stripes

**1.** Trim the selvage edges and sew 2 strips (for Size 1, use 1 full strip and 1 half strip), end to end, for each Solid 1 and Print 4 fabric. Repeat to make 2 long strips from each fabric. Cut the strips to length: 55″ for Size 1, or 73″ for Sizes 2 and 3.

**2.** Sew the strips to each side of the center column as shown in the assembly diagram below. Press the seams toward the center column and topstitch ⅛″ from the seams on top of the seam allowances.

# Finish the tablecloth

**1.** Sew the Solid 2 large rectangles to each side of the pieced center as shown in the assembly diagram. Press the seam allowances toward the stripes and topstitch ⅛″ from the seams on top of the seam allowances.

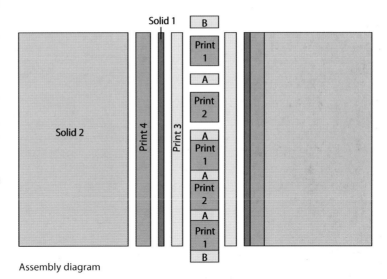

Assembly diagram

**2.** Hem (page 119) all 4 sides of the cloth by pressing under ½″, tucking the raw edges into the fold, and stitching ⅛″ from the edge.

You might be able to buy a hemming foot for your sewing machine. It's very useful in hemming long edges like those on this tablecloth, and it will definitely save you time.

*Arrange the cloth on your table and enjoy a beautiful meal.*

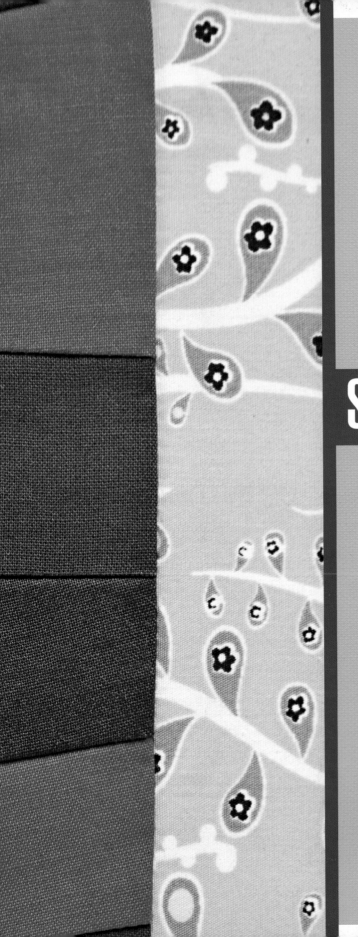

# Strips and Stripes

Adding strips of solids to highlight your gorgeous prints

## Materials

**Print 1:** ⅝ yard (for strap, interior pocket, and bottom insert)

**9 different prints:** ⅛ yard each (for exterior stripes)

**Solid 1:** ⅝ yard (for exterior stripes, straps, and tab)

**Solid 2:** ⅝ yard (for lining and interior pocket)

**Heavyweight interfacing** (I use Pellon 50): 1½ yards (for exterior foundation)

**Pressed cardboard:** 2 rectangles 3¼″ × 13½″ (for bottom insert)

**1″ cotton webbing:** 1½ yards (for straps)

**1 magnetic closure**

**Fine-point permanent marker**

**Erasable fabric marker**

### tip

To choose the 9 prints for the exterior of the bag, first select 2 prints of 2 different colors that will go on the ends of the bag. Then choose the other 7 prints, trying to find colors that blend from one end color to the other. Select colors that are all approximately the same value (page 10) so the only significant change is the color itself. For example, my gradation went from blue to greens to yellow-green.

# gradations bag

**FINISHED DIMENSION:** 13¾″ wide × 8″ tall × 3½″ deep, with 11″ straps

It's all about color—two of your favorite colors. This useful little bag is its own study on color theory. You choose print fabrics in two colors and then create a gradation, or spectrum, between them by finding more prints that blend from one to the other. Strips of these colors are foundation pieced onto heavyweight interfacing, forming the bag front and back. By separating the prints with neutral solid strips, you get to highlight the prints and colors *and* end up with a darling bag you'll want to carry every day.

## Cutting

**FROM PRINT 1:**

Cut 2 strips 1½″ × 25″

Cut 1 rectangle 11″ × 6″

Cut 1 rectangle 8⅛″ × 17″

From each of the 9 prints:

Cut 2 strips 2½″ × 11½″

From Solid 1:

Cut 7 strips 1½″ × width of fabric; crosscut into 20 strips 1½″ × 11½″

Cut 2 strips 1½″ × 25″

Cut 2 squares 5″ × 5″

From Solid 2:

Cut 1 strip 10¾″ × width of fabric; crosscut into 2 rectangles 19¼″ × 10¾″

Cut 1 rectangle 11″ × 6″

From interfacing:

Cut 4 rectangles 19¼″ × 10¾″

Cut 2 squares 5″ × 5″

# Construction

## Prepare the foundation pieces

**1.** Fold 2 interfacing rectangles in half along the long (19¼″) edge. Use the fold line to mark the center at the top and bottom edges with a permanent marker (Figure 1).

**2.** Mark 2½″ from each corner along the long top edge of the 2 interfacing rectangles. Cut a diagonal line from each 2½″ mark to its corresponding bottom corner (Figure 1).

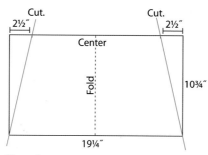

Figure 1

### NOTE

Both measuring and marking the lines accurately are very important if you want your two sides to match perfectly—so take your time. Use a fine-point permanent marker; the lines will be concealed by the seams, even if you use lighter fabrics.

**3.** Draw the seamlines on the 2 foundation pieces (Figure 2). Place marks along the right top edge, measuring from the center, at the following intervals: ½″, 1″, 2″, 2½″, 3½″, 4″, 5″, 5½″, and 6½″. Then mark the right bottom edge as follows: ¾″, 1¼″, 2¾″, 3¼″, 4¾″, 5¼″, 6¾″, 7¼″, and 8¾″. Draw a line from each top mark to its corresponding bottom mark. Repeat for the left side.

**4.** Cut out 2″ × 2″ notches from each of the bottom corners of both foundation pieces, as shown in Figure 3. The 2″ mark on the ruler should line up the same distance (approximately 2¼″) from each corner (Figure 4).

## Piece the bag exterior

You will be piecing the exteriors from the centers out, alternating between print and solid strips. The marked lines are on the back of the foundation pieces.

**1.** Lay out the 2½″ × 11½″ print strips so the colors blend from one end to the other (see Tip, page 39).

**2.** Take the center print strip and lay it, right side up, over the center fold on the front (unmarked) side of a foundation piece, positioning the strip so the edges cover the marked lines on each side of the center fold. If necessary, hold the pieces up to a light to do this.

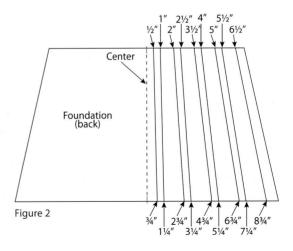

Figure 2

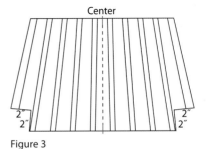

Figure 3

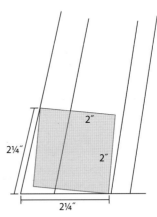

Figure 4

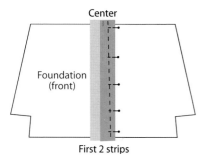

Center

Foundation
(front)

First 2 strips

Figure 5

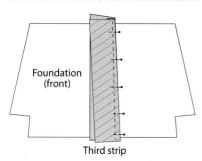

Foundation
(front)

Third strip

Figure 6

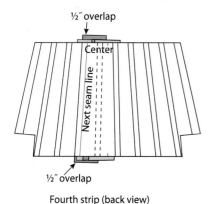

½" overlap

Center

Next seam line

½" overlap

Fourth strip (back view)

Figure 7

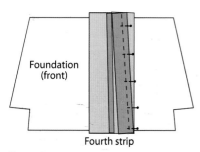

Foundation
(front)

Fourth strip

Figure 8

**3.** Lay a Solid 1 strip (1½˝ × 11½˝) on top of the center print strip, right sides together. Align the long raw edges with both strips overhanging the top and bottom of the foundation (see Figure 5). Pin in place.

**4.** Flip the foundation over (marked side) and sew along the marked line closest to the center and near the edges of the pinned fabric. From the front, trim the seam allowances to approximately ¼˝. Press the top strip toward the seam allowance.

**5.** Lay the next (print) strip on top of the last (solid) strip, right sides together. Align the top strip with the next seamline, following the angle of the line and overlapping it by about ½˝ (Figure 6). If necessary, flip to the back side to better adjust where the strip is positioned (Figure 7). Pin in place.

## tip

To better see the placement of the strips, you may find it helpful to trim the strips close to the foundation edge after you sew and press each one.

If you align the raw edge of the solid strips with the line after the next seamline, you will have a perfect ½˝ overlap.

**6.** Flip to the back and stitch along the seamline. From the front, trim the seam allowance to ¼˝. Press toward the seam allowance.

**7.** Repeat Steps 5 and 6, alternating between solid and print strips, until half of the foundation is covered. Repeat for the other half and the second foundation piece.

**8.** Trim the fabric strips even with the foundation edges.

# Assemble the bag exterior

**1.** Pin each of the 2 remaining interfacing rectangles to the back (marked side) of a foundation piece. Baste the layers ⅛″ from the foundation edges. Trim the interfacing to match the foundation, creating the exterior pieces.

**2.** Align and pin the 2 exterior pieces together, right sides together. Stitch with a ½″ seam along both sides and the bottom. Do not stitch the notched corners. Press the seams open.

**3.** "Pinch," sew, and trim each bottom corner to create a boxed corner (page 119).

**4.** Turn the exterior right side out.

# Make the lining

**1.** Refer to Prepare the Foundation Pieces, Step 2 (page 40), to cut the angled sides of the Solid 2 rectangles (19¼″ × 10¾″), and Step 4 (page 41), to cut the notched corners for the lining.

**2.** Align the Print 1 and Solid 2 rectangles (11″ × 6″), right sides together. Sew around the edges with a ½″ seam, leaving a 3″ opening in one long edge. Trim the corners at an angle and turn the pocket right side out through the opening. Press flat. Turn under the seam allowance of the opening and topstitch along that entire pocket edge to close.

**3.** Center the pocket to the right side of 1 lining piece, print fabric facing up, with the topstitched edge 3½″ from the top. Pin in place.

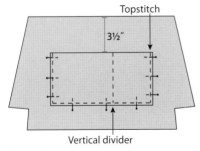

Topstitch

3½″

Vertical divider

Figure 9

**4.** Topstitch down the pocket sides and across the bottom, backstitching at both ends. Then topstitch one off-center vertical divider (Figure 9).

**5.** Align and pin the 2 lining pieces, right sides together. Stitch with a ½″ seam along both sides and the bottom, leaving a 5″ opening in the bottom. Do not sew the notched corners. Press the seams open.

**6.** "Pinch," sew, and trim each corner to make boxed corners (page 119).

## Make the straps and the tab

**1.** Sew a Solid 1 and Print 1 strip (each 1½″ × 25″), right sides together, along both long edges with ¼″ seams. Turn and press flat. Repeat to make 2 fabric tubes.

**2.** Cut 2 pieces 25″ long of cotton webbing; then pull 1 through each fabric tube. Adjust so the seams lie along the edges of the webbing.

**3.** Topstitch the straps ⅛″ from both long edges.

**4.** Mark ¼″ in from both short edges along the same long edge. Trim the strap ends at an angle from the unmarked corner to the ¼″ mark, as shown in Figure 10.

**5.** Mark ⅞″ from both top corners of a 5″ × 5″ interfacing square. Cut each side at an angle from a mark to the corresponding unmarked corner (Figure 11). Repeat for the other interfacing square.

**6.** Use the trimmed interfacing pieces to mark and trim the Solid 1 squares (5″ × 5″). Align and baste each interfacing piece to the back of a matching fabric piece using a ¼″ seam.

**7.** Follow the manufacturer's instructions to install 1 side of the magnetic closure onto the fabric side of an interfacing tab, positioning it centered and 1½″ from the bottom (wide) edge (Figure 11).

**8.** Align the 2 interfacing tabs, fabric sides together, and stitch around the 2 sides and bottom with a ½″ seam. Trim seam allowance to ¼″ and trim off corners (Figure 12).

**9.** Turn the tab right side out, using a turning tool to poke out the corners. Press flat. Topstitch around the sides and bottom ⅛″ from the edges.

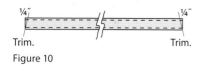

¼″         ¼″
Trim.        Trim.
Figure 10

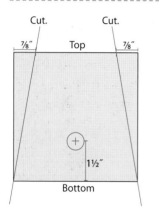

Cut.     Cut.
⅞″   Top   ⅞″
1½″
Bottom
Figure 11

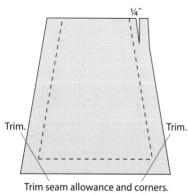

¼″
Trim.        Trim.
Trim seam allowance and corners.
Figure 12

# Complete the bag

**1.** Using an erasable marker, mark the top center of both the front and back sides of the bag exterior and lining.

**2.** Follow the manufacturer's instructions to attach the other half of the magnetic closure 2½" down from the center top edge of the bag exterior (front side).

**3.** Pin the ends of each strap, solid fabric facing down, to the bag exterior so that the corners of the untrimmed edge line up with the outside of the third solid stripe from the center print (Figure 13). Make sure the straps are not twisted. Baste ¼" from the edges. Repeat for the other side of the bag.

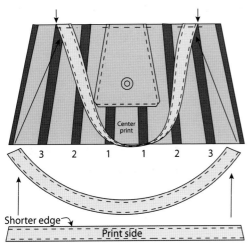

Figure 13

**4.** Pin the tab (magnetic closure facing up) centered on the back of the bag exterior, aligning the raw edges (Figure 13). Baste ¼" from the edge.

**5.** Insert the bag exterior into the lining, right sides together. Pin the top raw edges, matching the side seams and the centers, and making sure the straps and tab lie flat between the layers. Sew around the entire top with a ½" seam.

**6.** Pull the exterior through the hole in the bottom of the lining; then flip the lining inside of the bag. Press the seam flat. Topstitch ⅛" and again ¼" from the top edge. Hand stitch the lining opening closed.

**7.** Press under ¼", toward the wrong side on one short end of the Print 1 rectangle (8⅛" × 17"). Press under again and topstitch close to the edge.

**8.** Fold the hemmed rectangle in half lengthwise, right sides together. Sew around the rectangle with a ½" seam, leaving the hemmed end open. Trim the corner, turn right side out, and press the case flat.

**9.** Trim the corners of the 2 pressed cardboard rectangles slightly to remove the sharp points. Insert the cardboard into the case. Tuck the hemmed end of the case inside itself so the cardboard is covered and won't easily come out. Insert it into the bottom of the bag. Press the sides of the bag, using the first print fabrics as a guide, for a boxy look.

> **tip**
>
> If you like a very firm bag bottom, instead of using pressed cardboard to stabilize it, you can use pieces of ⅛"-thick hardboard (a type of fiberboard sometimes also called *lauan*). To trim it to size, you'll need to cut it with a saw.

**10.** If you choose to, add a decorative button or pin to the outside of the tab.

*Now you're ready to make a color statement.*

## Materials

**Prints 1, 2, and 3:** ⅜ yard each (for stripes)

**Prints 4 and 5:** ¼ yard each (for stripes)

**Solids 1, 2, 3, and 4:** ⅜ yard each (for stripes and vehicles)

**Solid 5, light:** ½ yard (for vehicle background)

**Solid 6, dark:** ⅛ yard (brown, or other dark, for wheels)

**Binding:** ½ yard for straight-grain binding (¾ yard for bias binding)

**Backing:** 2¾ yards

**Batting:** 1⅜ yards of 90″ wide (or packaged twin size)

**Steam-A-Seam 2 fusible web:** 3 sheets 9″ × 12″

**Fine-point permanent marker**

**Erasable fabric marker or chalk**

# traffic jam quilt

**FINISHED QUILT:** 40″ × 53⅞″

Beep! Beep! A traffic jam has never been so much fun. The appliquéd vehicles on this little boy's quilt have a retro vibe that keeps it from being too cutesy, so it easily makes the transition from baby to big boy. The oh-so-simple strip piecing is a great way to use novelty fabric, while the strips of solids keep your color scheme consistent.

## Cutting

**FROM PRINT 1:**

Cut 2 strips 2″ × 40″ [A, HH]

Cut 1 strip 3″ × 40″ [O]

Cut 1 strip 1¾″ × 40″ [Z]

**FROM PRINT 2:**

Cut 1 strip 2″ × 40″ [D]

Cut 1 strip 3¼″ × 40″ [M]

Cut 1 strip 2¼″ × 40″ [W]

Cut 1 strip 1⅝″ × 40″ [DD]

**FROM PRINT 3:**

Cut 2 strips 2½″ × 40″ [E, AA]

Cut 1 strip 2¾″ × 40″ [K]

Cut 1 strip 3″ × 40″ [T]

**FROM PRINT 4:**

Cut 2 strips 1⅝″ × 40″ [H, R]

Cut 1 strip 2⅜″ × 40″ [FF]

**FROM PRINT 5:**

Cut 2 strips 1⅛″ × 40″ [F, P]

Cut 1 strip 1¼″ × 40″ [X]

**FROM SOLID 1:**

Cut 2 strips 1¼″ × 40″ [B, L]

Cut 1 strip 1½″ × 40″ [V]

Cut 1 strip 1″ × 40″ [CC]

**FROM SOLID 2:**

Cut 1 strip 1¾″ × 40″ [C]

Cut 2 strips 1½″ × 40″ [J, BB]

Cut 1 strip 1¼″ × 40″ [N]

Cut 1 strip 1″ × 40″ [U]

**FROM SOLID 3:**

Cut 1 strip 1″ × 40″ [G]

Cut 1 strip 1¾″ × 40″ [Q]

Cut 1 strip 2″ × 40″ [Y]

Cut 1 strip 1⅛″ × 40″ [GG]

**FROM SOLID 4:**

Cut 2 strips 1¼″ × 40″ [I, EE]

Cut 1 strip 2″ × 40″ [S]

**FROM SOLID 5:**

Cut 2 strips 5½″ × 40″

# Construction

*All seams are a scant ¼″ unless otherwise noted.*

## Make the appliqué strips

*Templates are on pages 50 and 51.*

**1.** Use the templates to trace 2 copies of each vehicle piece onto Steam-a-Seam 2 with a fine-point permanent marker. The dashed lines indicate where one piece continues under another. Trace each piece (such as the wheels) separately. Windows are simply cut out, so trace them as part of the vehicle body.

**2.** Cut out each piece loosely outside the line. Peel off the unmarked side of the paper and stick (do not fuse) onto the wrong side of various solid fabrics. If desired, refer to the photo for vehicle color options. Then, cut out the shapes precisely on the lines through all layers. Remove the windows by carefully snipping the center of the window with pointed scissors, then inserting the scissors into the opening and cutting along the line.

**3.** Use an erasable fabric marker to draw a line 1½″ from the bottom long edge of each Solid 5 strip. Also mark ¾″ in from each short edge.

**4.** Peel off the paper backing from the vehicle pieces and position one of each vehicle type along a Solid 5 strip so that the bottom edge of their bodies lies on the marked line. Except for the camper trailer, do not put on the wheels yet. Evenly space the vehicles along the strip, with the left and right vehicles lying just inside the ¾″ end marks. The Steam-a-Seam 2 will temporarily keep them in place until they are fused. Refer to the quilt assembly diagram at right and the photo for placement options. Or arrange them as you desire.

**5.** Fuse the vehicle bodies in place permanently, following the manufacturer's directions.

**6.** Stitch around the edges of each vehicle with a matching thread. Use a zigzag stitch (with a short stitch length and narrow width) or a satin stitch if your machine has one. For a "raw" edge that will fray a little when washed, straight stitch near the edges instead.

**7.** Stick the wheels in place, using the pattern pieces as a guide. Fuse in place permanently.

**8.** Stitch around the edges of the wheels as in Step 6.

## tip

I use a tear-away stabilizer (usually used for embroidery) behind my appliqué when I'm zigzagging the edges. It's not required, but it helps keep everything flat and prevents the stitch from bunching the fabric. Just rip away the remaining stabilizer when you are finished.

# Complete the quilt

**1.** Use the quilt assembly diagram (below) as a guide to sew together the top, middle, and bottom strip-set sections with a ¼″ seam. All the strips are the same length, so both ends should be even. Pin as needed. Backstitch at both ends to secure them. Press all seam allowances to one side.

**2.** Add the appliqué strips between the strip-set sections. Press seam allowances away from appliqué strips.

**3.** Baste ⅛″ from all 4 outer edges of the quilt top to help secure them.

**4.** Refer to Quiltmaking Basics (pages 119-124) for directions on how to layer, baste, quilt, and bind your quilt.

*Here's hoping your little guy gets many years of enjoyment from it!*

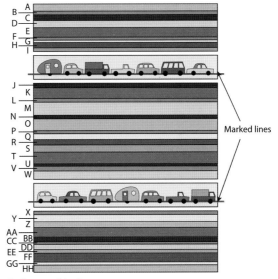

Quilt assembly diagram

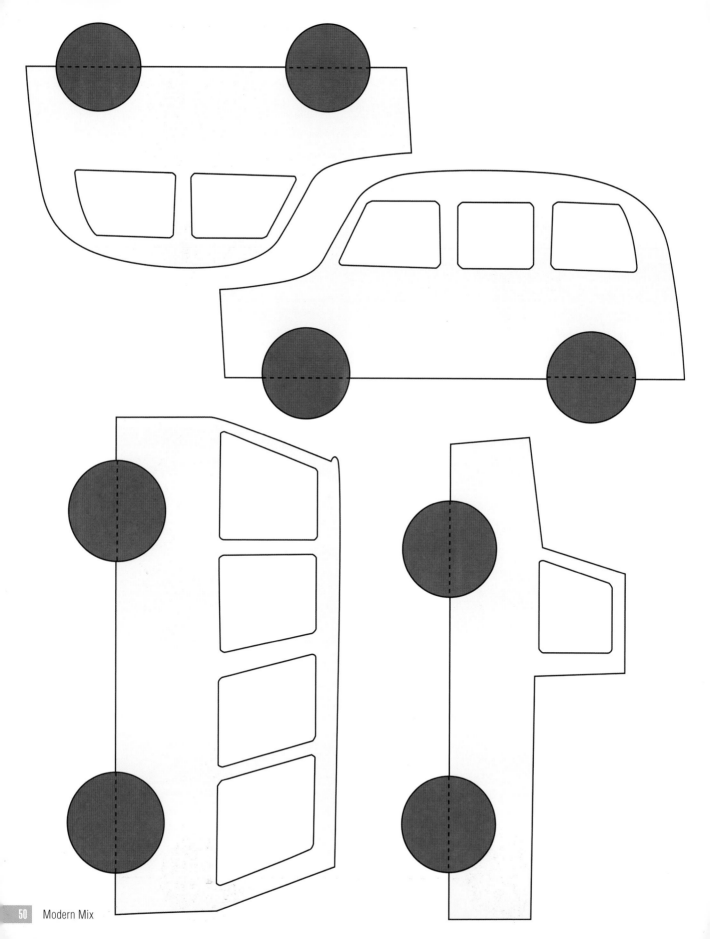

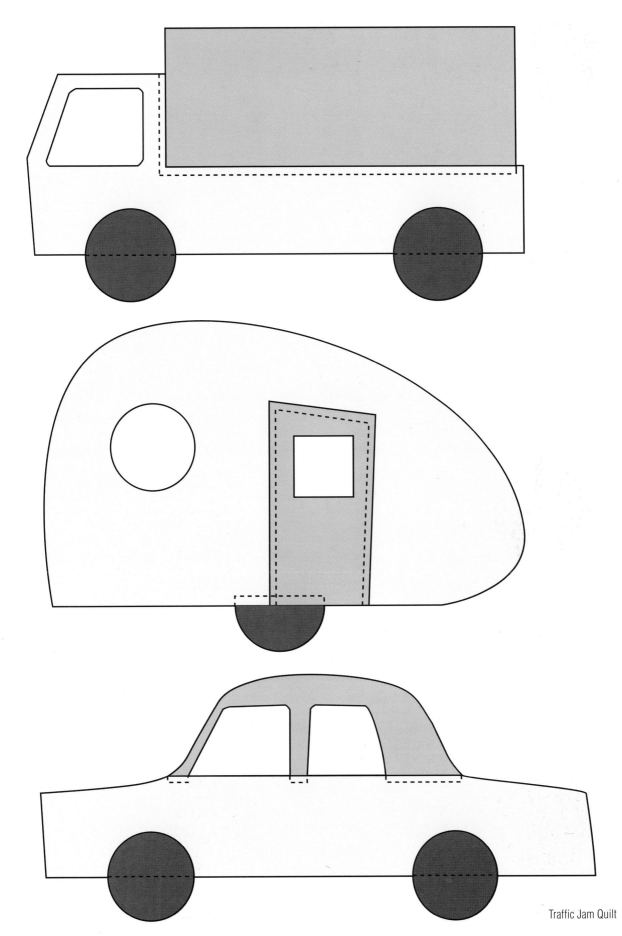

# stripe of strips pillow

**FINISHED SIZE:** 13½" square, 15½" square, or 17½" square

## Materials

**Print:** ⅝ yard (for main front and back body)

**Solid scraps:** enough to cover your muslin strip

**Muslin:** ¼ yard (for foundation)

**Square pillow form:** 14", 16", or 18"*

*The cover is sewn ½" smaller than the pillow form for a nice, firm pillow.

### tip

You can reverse the solid and print fabrics for a different look. I recommend that your scraps, whether solid or print, be analogous in color (see Design and Color, pages 9–11) to create a distinct stripe (not too "scrappy" looking).

This is a great project for using up some of your favorite small scraps. The scraps are pieced onto a muslin foundation, and you can use solid scraps with a print background or vice versa. Plus, make it in several sizes to fit your decor; you'll find instructions here for 14", 16", and 18" pillow forms. FYI: This quick and easy project makes a great gift!

## Cutting

|  | PRINT | MUSLIN |
|---|---|---|
| **14" pillow** | 2 strips 14½" × 5¾" [A]<br>2 rectangles 14½" × 9¾" [B] | 1 strip 14½" × 5" |
| **16" pillow** | 2 strips 16½" × 6½" [A]<br>2 rectangles 16½" × 11" [B] | 1 strip 16½" × 5½" |
| **18" pillow** | 2 strips 18½" × 7¼" [A]<br>2 rectangles 18½" × 12¼" [B] | 1 strip 18½" × 6" |

# Construction

*All seams are ½″ unless otherwise noted.*

## Piece the scrappy stripe

Choose scraps that are longer than the width of your muslin strip. I used varying widths from ¾″ to 2½″. You can cut the scraps to size as you sew.

**1.** Lay the first scrap, right side up, on the end of the muslin strip so it hangs over 3 edges. Lay the second scrap, right side down, along the raw edge of the first scrap (Figure 1). It should hang over the top and bottom edges of the muslin.

**2.** Stitch through all layers with an approximate ¼″ seam (Figure 1). The width of the seam is not critical. The sewn line should be straight but does not have to be perfectly perpendicular to the muslin strip. It's even great if the seam is at a different angle than the raw edges of the scraps.

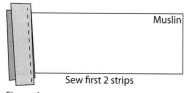

Muslin

Sew first 2 strips

Figure 1

**3.** Trim the seam allowance to approximately ¼˝. Press the top scrap toward the seam.

**4.** Lay the next scrap, right side down, along the edge of the previous one. Stitch with a randomly angled seam (Figure 2). Press toward seam.

**5.** Repeat Step 4 until the muslin strip is entirely covered.

**6.** Flip the strip over and baste ¼˝ from the muslin edge (Figure 3). Trim the overhanging scraps even with the edges of the muslin strip.

## Assemble the pillow front and back

**1.** Sew a strip [A] onto the top and bottom of the muslin strip, right sides together, with a ½˝ seam to make the pillow front. Press the seam allowances toward the pieced strip (Figure 4).

**2.** Hem (page 119) each rectangle [B] by pressing under ½˝ along one long edge. Tuck the raw edges into the fold and press again. Topstitch ⅛˝ from the folded edge.

**3.** Lay the hemmed rectangles [B] on top of each other, right sides facing up, overlapping the hems to create a square the same size as the front (14½˝, 16½˝, or 18½˝). Pin in place and baste along the sides ¼˝ from the edges (Figure 5).

## Complete the pillow

**1.** Pin the pillow front and back together, right sides together. Stitch around all 4 sides with a ½˝ seam. Trim the corners at an angle and turn right side out through the back opening.

**2.** Insert the pillow form through the opening in the back.

*Get comfy and enjoy!*

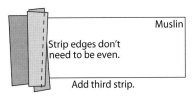

Muslin

Strip edges don't need to be even.

Add third strip.

Figure 2

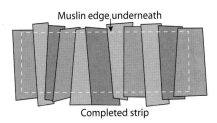

Muslin edge underneath

Completed strip

Figure 3

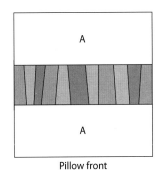

A

A

Pillow front

Figure 4

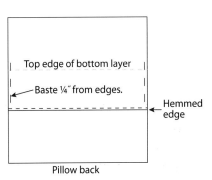

Top edge of bottom layer

Baste ¼˝ from edges.

Hemmed edge

Pillow back

Figure 5

## Materials

**Light Solid 1:** ⅝ yard
(for pieced sections and Border 1)

**5–7 additional light solids:** ¼ yard
each (for pieced sections)

**9 dark prints:** ⅜ yard each
(for stripes and Border 2)

**Medium Print 1:** ¾ yard (for Border 3)

**3 additional medium prints:**
¼ yard each (for stripes)

**Backing:** 3⅜ yards

**Binding:** ½ yard for straight-grain
binding (¾ yard for bias binding)

**Batting:** 1¾ yards of 90″ wide
(or packaged twin size)

## Cutting

**FROM LIGHT SOLID 1:**

Cut 6 strips 1¼″ × width of fabric (for Border 1)
Save leftovers to use with light solids (below)

**FROM EACH LIGHT SOLID:**

Cut 3 strips 2″ × width of fabric

Crosscut these strips to various random
lengths between 1½″ and 13″

**FROM EACH DARK PRINT:**

Cut 1 strip 2″ × width of fabric (for Border 2)

Cut 3 strips of varied sizes between 1¼″ and
3″ × width of fabric; do not trim selvage edges

**FROM MEDIUM PRINT 1:**

Cut 6 strips 3¼″ × width of fabric (for Border 3).
Save leftovers to use with medium prints (below)

**FROM EACH MEDIUM PRINT:**

Cut 2 strips of varied sizes between 1″ and
2¼″ × width of fabric; do not trim selvage edges

# boyfriend quilt

**FINISHED QUILT:** approximately 52″ × 71¼″

A simple, masculine quilt for the guy in your life. The print strips are cut across the width of the fabric, which makes for some quick piecing. The solid sections use random lengths of various shades of one color to add interest without looking fussy. If you want to make it an extra-special gift, add some personalization. I personalized my quilt by embroidering the recipient's name across a strip on the back (page 59).

# Construction

*All seams are a scant ¼˝ unless otherwise noted.*

## Sew the light pieced sections

**1.** Sew together strips of the 2˝ light solid strips end to end with a ¼˝ seam, alternating colors and lengths at random, until the strip is longer than 43˝. Press the seam allowances to one side. Repeat to make 13 strips of this length.

**2.** Sew the pieced strips together along their long edges to make 3 sections; 2 sections will have 4 strips and one will have 5 (see quilt assembly diagram, right). When sewing, line up the ends of the strips along one edge, so that this one edge is even. Press seam allowances to one side.

## Sew striped sections

**1.** Sew the medium and dark strips together into 4 strip-set sections [A, B, C, and D] with a ¼˝ seam as shown in the quilt assembly diagram. When sewing, line up the selvage ends of the strips along one edge, so that this one edge is even. Choose the strips randomly in both fabric and height and include 1 or 2 of the medium fabrics in each section. Continue adding strips until the height measurements of each section are approximately as follows: [A] = 7¾˝, [B] = 16˝, [C] = 11˝, and [D] = 8½˝.

> If you go over the height dimension, you can trim the section down after sewing, but it isn't necessary that yours are exactly the same as mine.

**2.** Press seam allowance to one side; then trim off the selvage edges on the even edge, making sure to trim perpendicular to the strips.

## Complete the construction

**1.** Sew together the sections with a ¼˝ seam as shown in the quilt assembly diagram. The 5-strip light section goes in the middle. Line up the even edges so that one side of the quilt top remains even. Press the seam allowances away from the light sections.

**2.** Trim down the long, uneven edge to the length of the smallest strip, making sure the quilt top is square.

**3.** Piece together 1 long strip 2˝ × 240˝ using the remaining dark print strips for Border 2. Cut the strips 2˝ wide and into varying lengths from 2˝ to 15˝ as they are sewn together end to end. Press the seam allowances to one side.

**4.** Add the 3 borders, referring to the quilt assembly diagram and Quiltmaking Basics (pages 119–120) for how to sew on borders.

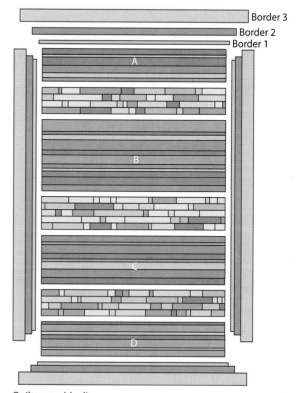

Quilt assembly diagram

**5.** Refer to Quiltmaking Basics (pages 121-124) for directions on how to layer, baste, quilt, and bind your quilt.

*I hope he likes it!*

Detail of quilt back

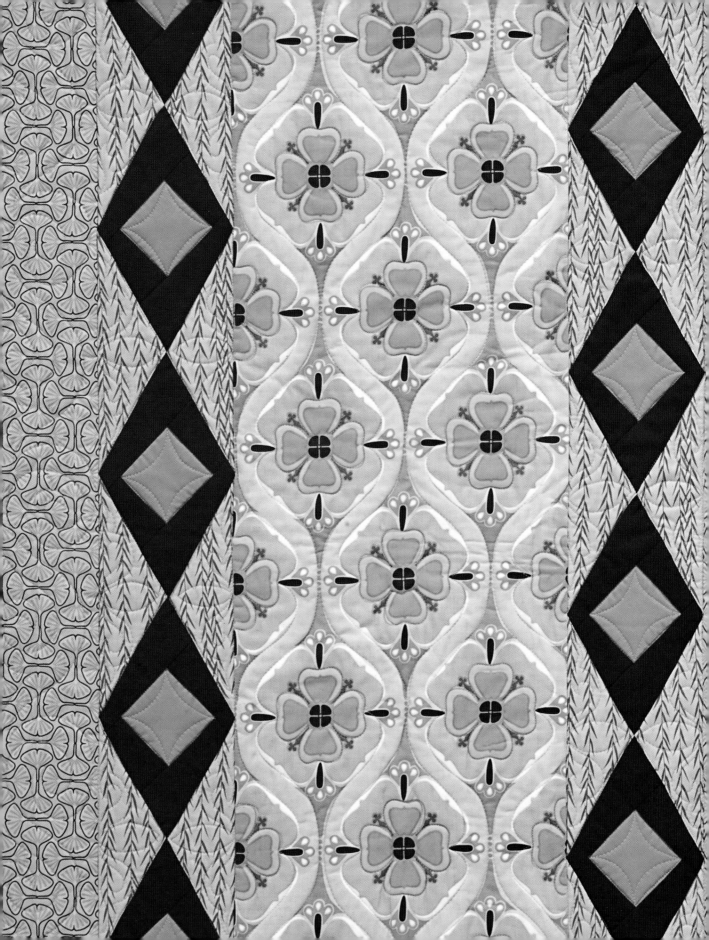

# Accentuate the Positive

Little bits of solid colors to bring out the best in patterns

## Materials

*The fabrics listed are for one twin-size quilt.*

**12 prints:** ⅝ yard each (analogous colors for the blocks) or plenty of scraps from your stash (some must be 20″–25″ long)

**Solid 1:** 1⅞ yards (for block contrast stripe)

**Solid 2:** 1 yard (for block contrast strips and triangles)

**Muslin:** 6 yards (36″–40″ wide)*

**Binding:** ⅝ yard for straight-grain binding (⅞ yard for bias binding)

**Backing:** 6¼ yards

**Batting:** 3 yards of 90″ wide (or packaged queen size)

**Long cutting ruler or yardstick**

**Large square cutting ruler** (12″ × 12″ or bigger)

**Erasable fabric marker or fine-point permanent marker**

*\*If you're using white or very light fabrics, use bleached white muslin.*

# twin string quilt

**FINISHED BLOCK:** 17″ × 17″

**FINISHED QUILT:** 68½″ × 102½″

Here's a perfect pair of twin quilts that coordinate but aren't identical. These string quilts are foundation pieced onto muslin and use random-width strips. Using lots of different prints in the same color family adds depth and personality, while the solids tie it all together. The solid strips in each block are arranged to create a strong pattern that is revealed only after you assemble all the blocks into rows. Break out your stash of scraps and add some new prints to make it all work together.

# Cutting

## FROM PRINT FABRICS:

From each fabric, cut 13 strips across the width of fabric, as follows:

3 strips at 1¼˝

2 strips each at 1˝, 1½˝, 1¾˝, and 2˝

1 strip each at 2¼˝ and 2½˝

The width of the strips need not be exact because we are trying to achieve a random look. For an even more "wonky" look, cut the strips at uneven widths or sew them crooked onto the foundation. So, it's all right to work with the scraps you have, no matter what width they are.

## NOTE

If you are combining scraps with yardage, you need a total of:

36 strips at 1¼˝

24 strips each at 1˝, 1½˝, 1¾˝, and 2˝

12 strips each at 2¼˝ and 2½˝

## FROM SOLID 1:

Remove the selvage edge and refer to the cutting diagram below to cut 24 strips as follows:

22 strips 3⅝˝ × 26˝ along the length of the fabric

2 strips 3⅝˝ × 26˝ across the width of the fabric

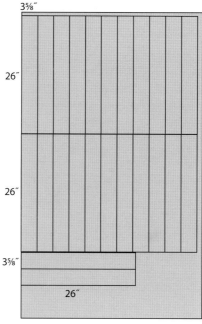

Cutting diagram

## FROM SOLID 2:

Cut 2 strips 5˝ × width of fabric; crosscut into 12 squares 5˝ × 5˝; cut each square diagonally to make 2 half-square triangles (24 total) for the corner triangles

Cut 8 strips 2½˝ × width of fabric; crosscut into 24 strips 2½˝ × 11½˝ for the corner contrast strips

## FROM MUSLIN:

Cut 24 squares 17½˝ × 17½˝

# Construction

*All seams are a scant ¼″ unless otherwise noted.*

## Mark and piece the blocks

Each block has a central diagonal stripe of a high-contrast solid fabric (Solid 1), one corner triangle of another solid fabric (Solid 2), and one corner with a solid contrast strip (Solid 2).

**1.** Mark 5 lines at 45° angles on each muslin square as shown in Figure 1. Use an erasable fabric marker or draw faintly with a fine-point permanent marker. Flip to the other side and draw a line as shown in Figure 2, making sure the angle is the same as the other side. The side with the 5 lines is the back.

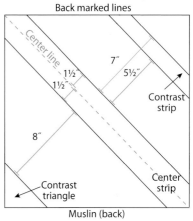

Back marked lines

Center line

7″

1½″

5½″

1½″

Contrast strip

8″

Contrast triangle

Center strip

Muslin (back)

Figure 1

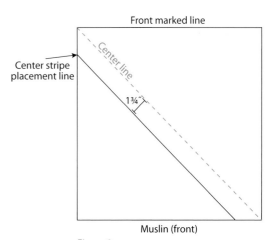

Front marked line

Center stripe placement line

Center line

1¾″

Muslin (front)

Figure 2

As you piece all the strips, you don't need to cut them down to size until after they are sewn on. Simply let the extra hang off one end of the muslin square and trim it later.

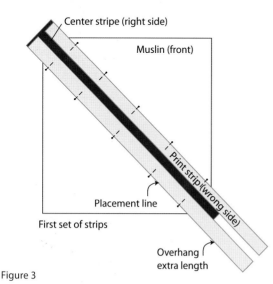

Center stripe (right side)

Muslin (front)

Print strip (wrong side)

Placement line

First set of strips

Overhang extra length

Figure 3

Trimmed larger than muslin

Muslin (front)

Print strip (wrong side)

Second set of strips

Overhang extra length

Figure 4

**2.** Lay a Solid 1 contrast stripe (3⅝˝ × 26˝), right side up, diagonally across the front of a muslin square. Position the stripe so that one raw edge lines up with the marked line and overhangs the corners evenly (Figure 3).

**3.** Position 1 print strip (any width greater than 1˝), right side down, on top of the contrast stripe. Align the long raw edges with the print strip overhanging the edge of the square a little (Figure 3). Pin. Repeat on the other edge of the contrast stripe with another print strip.

**4.** Flip to the back and sew along the 2 center marked lines. From the front, press the top strip toward the seam allowance. Roughly trim the excess fabric strips so that they only slightly overhang the muslin square.

**5.** Pin 2 more print strips (these can be any width), right side down, on top of the first strips so that the long raw edges line up and the new strips overhang the edge of the square a little (Figure 4). From the front, sew ¼˝ from the edges through all layers. Open, press, and trim as in Step 4.

**6.** Repeat Step 5, choosing print strips of varied widths and fabrics, until the next marked line (on the back) is covered by at least ¼˝. The widths of the strips aren't critical, so adjust the seam width if desired. Vary the widths to get about 6–9 strips per side. If the marked line is overlapped by more than ½˝, carefully trim the excess width of the last strip so that it overlaps only ¼˝ to ½˝.

After the first couple of blocks, be sure to use the shorter pieces you've trimmed off from previous strips to fill in the shorter sections. You want to make sure you'll still have some long pieces left for the last blocks. It's like a fun puzzle—trying to find strips that fit.

## COMPLETE THE CORNERS

On one side you will reach a single marked line for the corner contrast triangle, and on the other side you will reach two lines for the corner contrast strips. Each side will be completed as follows.

**On the triangle side:**

**1.** Pin a Solid 2 triangle on top of the print strip so that the diagonal edge lines up with the raw edge of the print strip and it overhangs each side evenly (Figure 5). Flip to the back and sew along the marked line. From the front, press the triangle toward the corner.

**On the strip side:**

**2.** Pin a Solid 2 contrast strip on top of the last print strip so that the long raw edges line up and it overhangs each side evenly. If the print strip doesn't evenly overlap the line, use the marked line (from the back) to adjust the contrast strip so that it evenly overlaps the line as shown in Figure 6. Flip to the back and sew along the marked line. From the front, press the strip toward the seam allowance.

**3.** Pin the next print strip, right side down, on top of the contrast strip so that the long raw edges line up and it overhangs each side. Flip to the back and sew along the next marked line. From the front, press the strip toward the seam allowance.

**4.** Continue adding print strips, as before, until the corner is covered. Try to vary the widths to get about 2–3 strips in this little section.

**5.** Trim the complete block even with the muslin square.

**6.** Repeat the entire process to make a total of 24 blocks.

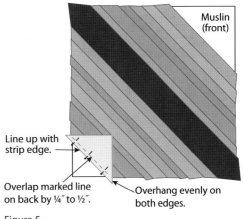

Muslin (front)

Line up with strip edge.

Overlap marked line on back by ¼″ to ½″.

Overhang evenly on both edges.

Figure 5

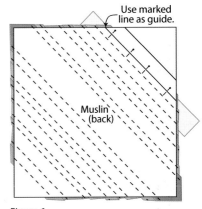

Use marked line as guide.

Muslin (back)

Figure 6

**tip**

Using a very large square ruler (12″ or greater—I used a 16″ ruler) will help you to trim the blocks so that the corners are all square. With all the piecing, the blocks may become distorted. Center the ruler the best you can on the block and trim evenly along all 4 sides.

# Complete the quilt

**1.** Use the quilt assembly diagram below as a guide to carefully arrange the 6 rows forming the overall diagonal pattern. Note that the rotation of the squares makes up the pattern of the quilt.

**2.** Sew the 6 rows of 4 blocks together. Press the seams in opposite directions.

**3.** Refer to Quiltmaking Basics (pages 119-124) for directions on how to layer, baste, quilt, and bind your quilt.

*Now make another so you have a matching pair!*

Quilt assembly diagram

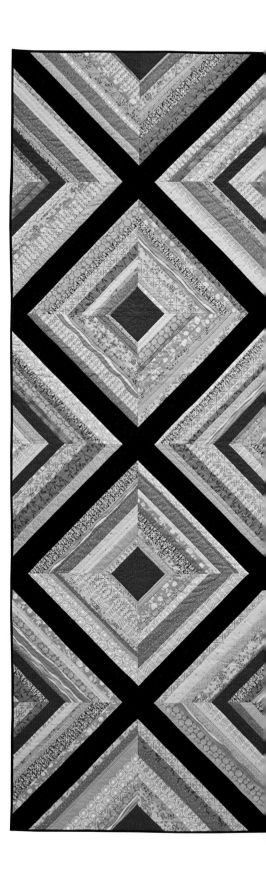

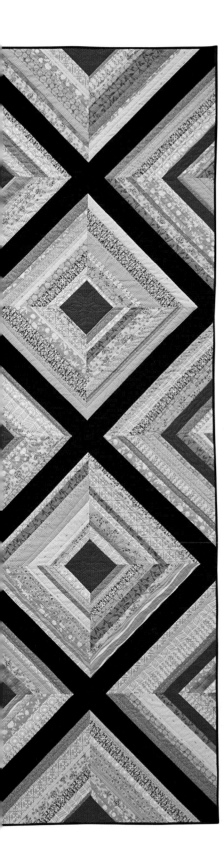
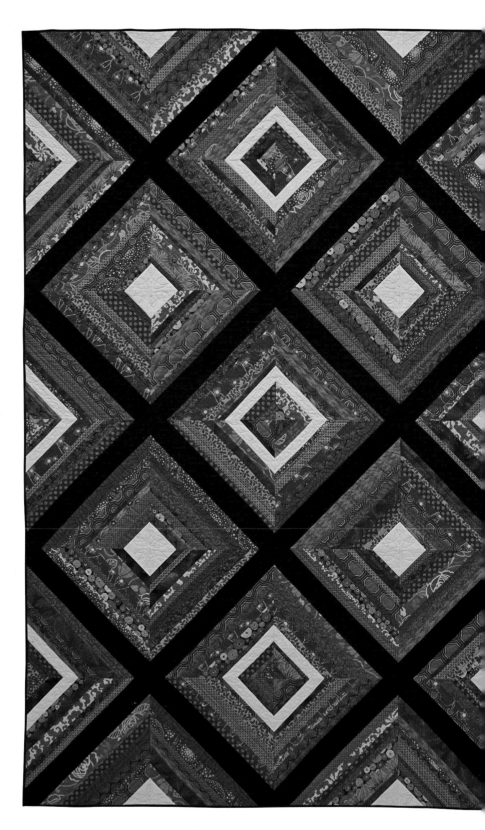

# quilted camera case

**FINISHED SIZE:** varies depending on your camera

## Materials

**Print 1:** a scrap at least 10″ × 8″ (for case exterior)

**Print 2:** a scrap at least 8″ × 6″ (for tab)

**Solid 1:** a scrap at least 10″ × 10″
   (for strap and lining)

**Thin cotton batting:** a scrap at least 10″ × 8″

**Mid-weight sew-in interfacing:**
   a scrap at least 4″ × 6″

**Erasable marker**

This case was designed for your small point-and-shoot camera, but it works equally well for a phone. It will keep either device free of scratches as it floats around in a larger bag. The case features a couple prints you love with a solid strap for a pop of contrast color. It's custom made to fit the measurements of your own camera.

# Measuring

To make the case fit your specific camera, you'll need to do some measuring and a bit of math. Please don't be intimidated. Just sit down with the camera, a ruler, a calculator, and pen and paper—and take your time.

Using Figure 1 as a guide, measure your camera's length [A], height [B], and depth [C], and write these numbers down. Include the lens that might stick out. Because a little extra room is accounted for, you can round your measurements down to the nearest ⅛".

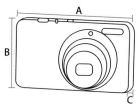

Figure 1

Now use the formulas to make a few calculations. Write down each number as you go. Round to the nearest ⅛".

## Cutting

*Use your measurements and calculations for sizes.*

**FROM PRINT 1:**
Cut 2 rectangles [H × G] (for exterior)

**FROM PRINT 2:**
Cut 2 rectangles 4¼" × [K] (for tab)

**FROM SOLID 1**
Cut 2 rectangles [H × G]; then trim ⅛" off the length and width (for lining). The lining is cut slightly smaller so it will fit neatly inside the camera case when assembled.

Cut 1 strip 1½" × [J] (for strap)

**FROM BATTING:**
Cut 2 rectangles [H × G]

**FROM INTERFACING:**
Cut 1 rectangle 4¼" × [K]

|  | FORMULA | YOUR CALCULATIONS | EXAMPLE |  |
|---|---|---|---|---|
| **A =** | Length |  | 3⅝" |  |
| **B =** | Height |  | 2¼" |  |
| **C =** | Depth |  | ¾" |  |
| **D =** | C ÷ 2 |  | ¾" ÷ 2 = | ⅜" |
| **E =** | 2 × B |  | 2 × 2¼" = | 4½" |
| **F =** | 2 × C |  | 2 × ¾" = | 1½" |
| **G =** | A + D + 1" |  | 3⅝" + ⅜" + 1" = | 5" |
| **H =** | B + C + ¾" |  | 2¼" + ¾" + ¾" = | 3¾" |
| **I =** | D + ⅛" |  | ⅜" + ⅛" = | ½" |
| **J =** | E + F + 1½" |  | 4½" + 1½" + 1½" = | 7½" |
| **K =** | B + ½" |  | 2¼" + ½" = | 2¾" |

# Construction

*All seams are ¼″ unless otherwise noted.*

## Sew the strap and exterior

**1.** Pin a batting rectangle to the wrong side of each Print 1 rectangle (exterior). Quilt these rectangles, sewing across in any pattern you'd like. I chose random slanted lines along the length.

**2.** Use the calculation [I] to mark and then trim off a square at 2 bottom corners (short side) of each quilted exterior (Figure 1).

**3.** Press the strap in half along its length. Open, press one short end in ¼″, and press (Figure 2). Fold in each of the long raw edges to meet at the center (Figure 3). Press again. Then fold in half again on the previous crease and press one last time.

**4.** Topstitch the strap close to both long edges, starting and stopping 1″ from the short edges (Figure 4).

**5.** Form a circle with the strap, making sure not to twist it. Tuck the raw end into the pressed end so that it overlaps by ½″ (Figure 5). Pin in place.

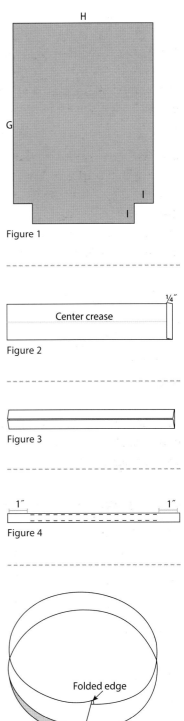

Figure 1

Figure 2

Figure 3

Figure 4

Figure 5

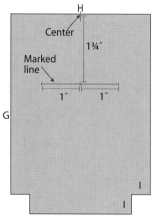

Figure 6

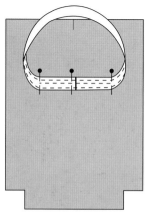

Figure 7

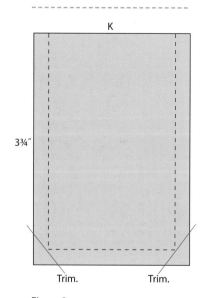

Figure 8

**6.** Use an erasable marker to mark the top center of one quilted exterior and again 1¾″ down from that. Then mark a line that extends 1″ to either side of the 1¾″ center mark (Figure 6).

**7.** Pin the strap onto the marked quilted exterior so that the overlapped edge is centered on the marked line. Also pin the strap at the 1″ marks on either side of the center (Figure 7). Topstitch the strap from one end-pin to the other, sewing along both sides of the strap and keeping close to the edges. Topstitch again through the strap center.

**8.** Align, right sides together, the 2 quilted exterior rectangles, keeping the strap between the layers but free of the seams. Sew the rectangles together along both sides and the bottom, using a ¼″ seam. Do not sew the notched corners. Press the seams open as much as possible.

## tip

When pressing small, awkward objects, try using either a pressing roll or a small towel rolled up, inserted inside the object. This allows you to press only the seam and not leave creases elsewhere.

**9.** "Pinch," sew, and trim each bottom corner to create a boxed corner (page 119). Turn the quilted exterior right side out.

## Sew the lining and the tab

**1.** Use the calculation [I] to mark and then trim off a square at 2 bottom corners (short side) of each lining rectangle (Figure 1).

**2.** Sew the lining rectangles, right sides together, along both sides and the bottom, leaving a 1½″ opening along the bottom center. Do not sew the notched corners. Press the seams open (see Tip above).

**3.** "Pinch," sew, and trim each bottom corner to create a boxed corner (page 119). Do not turn it right side out.

**4.** Align the 2 Print 2 tab rectangles, right sides together. Center the interfacing rectangle to one side of the layered fabric rectangles. Pin together. Sew along 3 sides, leaving a short [K] side open (Figure 8). Trim the corners and turn right side out. Press.

**5.** Topstitch close to the side and bottom edges.

# Complete the case

**1.** Pin the tab centered along the top edge of the exterior (on the side the strap is sewn onto) with right sides together and raw edges aligned. Insert the exterior into the lining, right sides together, keeping the tab between the layers. Align the raw edges and side seams and then pin.

**2.** Sew around the top edge with a ¼″ seam. This is the trickiest part. Be careful to keep the other side of the opening free when sewing through all the layers of one side. To do this, sew a few stitches, readjust the case under the presser foot, and continue sewing a few more stitches. Continue this way all the way around the top edge.

**3.** Pull the exterior through the opening in the bottom of the lining. Hand stitch the opening closed, and then push the lining into the exterior.

**4.** Topstitch close to the top edge, keeping the tab open and free, carefully stitching around the edge as before. Flip the strap around so that it surrounds the case.

*Now slip in your camera, tuck in the tab, and go!*

# diamond strands quilt

FINISHED DIAMOND: approximately 4⅛″ × 7⅛″

FINISHED QUILT: 59⅛″ × 74½″

## Materials

**Solid 1:** 1⅛ yards (for diamonds)

**Solid 2:** ⅜ yard (for diamond centers)

**Print 1 (small scale):** 1½ yards
  (for behind the diamonds)

**Prints 2, 3, and 4:** 2⅜ yards each
  (for long columns and backing)

**Binding:** ⅝ yard for straight-grain
  (¾ yard for bias binding)

**Backing:** pieced from leftover
  Prints 2, 3, and 4 (or 3¾ yards)

**Batting:** 2 yards of 90″-wide cotton
  batting (or packaged twin size)

**Clear template plastic:** 1 sheet
  8½″ × 11″ (minimum)

**Permanent marker**

This large lap quilt is perfect for using some of those larger-scale prints you love. The pieced diamonds add intricacy, but because they're pieced from solids, the result doesn't look too busy. And by using the remaining print fabric to piece the back, you aren't stuck with a lot of leftover fabric.

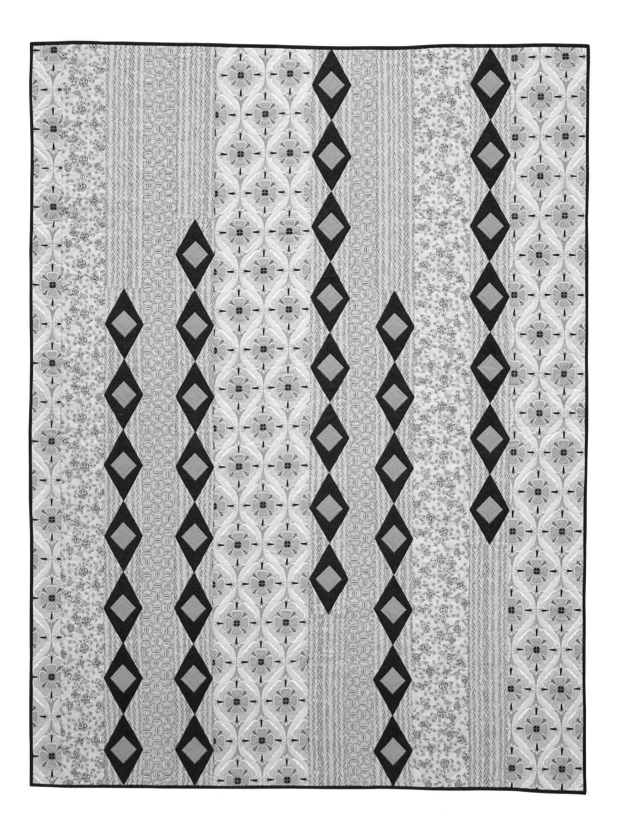

## Cutting

**FROM SOLID 1:**

Cut 18 strips 2⅛″ × width of fabric; crosscut 5 of these into 74 rectangles 2⅛″ × 2½″; crosscut the remaining 13 strips into 74 rectangles 2⅛″ × 5¾″

**FROM SOLID 2:**

Cut 3 strips 2½″ × width of fabric; crosscut these into 37 squares 2½″ × 2½″ for diamond center square

**FROM PRINT 1:**

Cut 4 strips 4⅝″ × width of fabric; crosscut these into

3 rectangles 4⅝″ × 25″ [C]

2 rectangles 4⅝″ × 18″ [E]

Save the remaining fabric for the diamond units.

**FROM PRINT 2:**

Trim one selvage edge; then from the *length* of the fabric

Cut 1 strip 3½″ × 74½″ [A]

Cut 1 strip 10¾″ × 74½″ [F]

Cut 1 strip 8½″ × 74½″ [I]

**FROM PRINT 3:**

Trim one selvage edge; then from the *length* of the fabric

Cut 1 strip 5″ × 74½″ [B]

Cut 1 strip 6½″ × 74½″ [H]

**FROM PRINT 4:**

Trim one selvage edge; then from the *length* of the fabric

Cut 1 strip 4″ × 74½″ [D]

Cut 1 strip 3¼″ × 74½″ [G]

## Construction

*All seams are a scant ¼″ unless otherwise noted.*

## Prepare and sew the diamonds

*Templates are on page 83.*

**1.** Using a permanent marker, trace the large [T1] and small [T2, T3] triangle templates onto template plastic (including the arrows) and cut out along the outer edges.

**2.** Trace the templates onto the right side of Print 1 and cut 64 large triangles [T1] and 10 each of the 2 small triangles [T2, T3].

### NOTE

If you are using a directional fabric as I did, you must pay attention to how you place your templates. Up and down arrows are marked on each triangle. If your fabric has a clear top and bottom, then you must cut half of your triangles with one end of the arrow up and the other half with the other end of the arrow up. This applies to both large and small triangles. But if the fabric design has no real direction, you don't need to worry about it.

**3.** Align and sew the 2½″ edges of 2 Solid 1 rectangles (2½″ × 2⅛″) to opposite sides of a Solid 2 diamond center square (2½″ × 2½″), using a scant ¼″ seam. Press seam allowances toward the darker fabric.

**4.** Align and sew a 5¾″ edge of a Solid 1 strip (5¾″ × 2⅛″) to each of the remaining 2 sides of the diamond center. Press seam allowances toward the darker fabric. This creates a "square within a square" block that will be trimmed to a diamond shape (see Figure 1).

**5.** Repeat Steps 3 and 4 to make a total of 37 "square within a square" units.

Refer to Quiltmaking Basics (page 119) and try chain piecing these squares. It will go much faster!

**6.** Trace the diamond template onto clear template plastic (including the diamond center). Cut out only along the outer edge of the template.

**7.** Position the diamond template onto a sewn square as shown in Figure 1, lining up the diamond center. Trace the template; then cut by hand or use a ruler and rotary cutter to cut the diamond piece along the line. Repeat to make 37 pieced diamonds.

## Make the diamond units and columns

**1.** Sew 2 large triangles [T1] to opposite sides of a pieced diamond, right sides together, as shown in Figure 2. One squared-off point of the triangle will line up with the edge of the diamond. Press seam allowances toward darker fabric. When pressed it will look like Figure 3. Repeat to make 27 diamond units.

### NOTE
For directional fabric, make sure that when opened up, both triangles have the fabric facing the same direction.

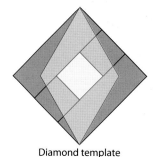

Diamond template
Figure 1

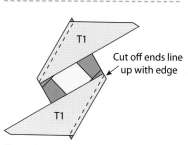

Cut off ends line up with edge

Figure 2

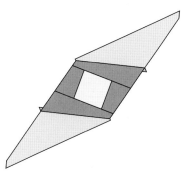

Figure 3

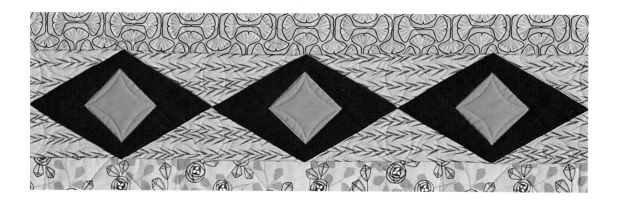

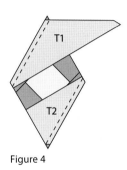
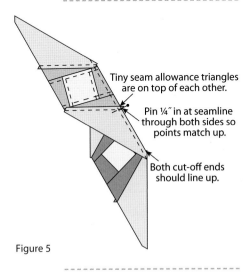

Figure 4

Tiny seam allowance triangles are on top of each other.

Pin ¼″ in at seamline through both sides so points match up.

Both cut-off ends should line up.

Figure 5

Line up this corner.

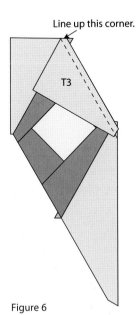

Figure 6

**2.** Sew a large triangle [T1] and a small triangle [T2] on opposite sides of one of the remaining pieced diamonds as shown in Figure 4. Press seam allowances toward darker fabric. Repeat to make a total of 10 diamond end units.

### NOTE

For directional fabric, sew half of the diamonds with the small triangle on the right, as shown, and the other half with it on the left, so that the fabric in both cases goes from top to bottom. Make sure that the larger triangle matches this direction.

**3.** Sew 2 of the diamond units together as shown in Figure 5. The cut-off point of the triangles should line up with the other unit's edge. Press seam allowances to one side.

### tip

If you want to be sure your diamond points meet perfectly, measure ¼″ in from the seam edge on both pieces and poke a pin through where that measurement crosses the seam on both pieces. Pin the pieces in place. With a ¼″ seam, this will be the spot where the seams meet exactly.

**4.** Continue to sew units together, referring to the diamond column assembly diagram (page 82), and adding a diamond end unit to each end of a column. Make 5 columns, 3 with 7 diamonds and 2 with 8 diamonds. Press seam allowances to one side.

**5.** Add a small triangle [T3] to the top and bottom as shown in Figure 6 to complete the column.

**6.** Refer to the quilt assembly diagram (page 82) to add a rectangle [C] or [E] to the top or bottom of each diamond column. Press seam allowance toward the rectangle.

**7.** Measure each column, being careful not to stretch it, and trim off enough of the rectangle end [C or E] to make the entire column measure exactly 74½″.

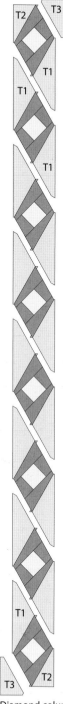

Diamond column
assembly diagram

# Complete the quilt

**1.** Refer to the quilt assembly diagram below to sew together the diamond columns to the plain print fabric columns. Backstitch at both ends for stability. Press seam allowances to one side.

**2.** Piece the backing from the remaining pieces of Prints 2, 3, and 4. Cut the pieces to about 82½" in length. There is no need to measure the width unless you want to. Just make sure the pieces are straight and even. Sew the 3 pieces together along the length, and you will have a backing that is more than wide enough.

**3.** Refer to Quiltmaking Basics (page 119-124) to layer, baste, quilt, and bind your quilt.

*All done!*

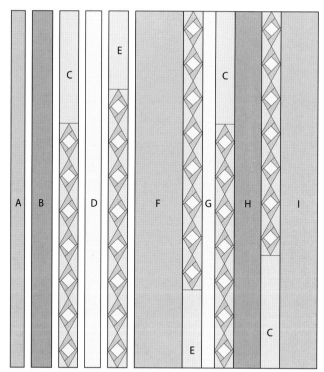

Quilt assembly diagram

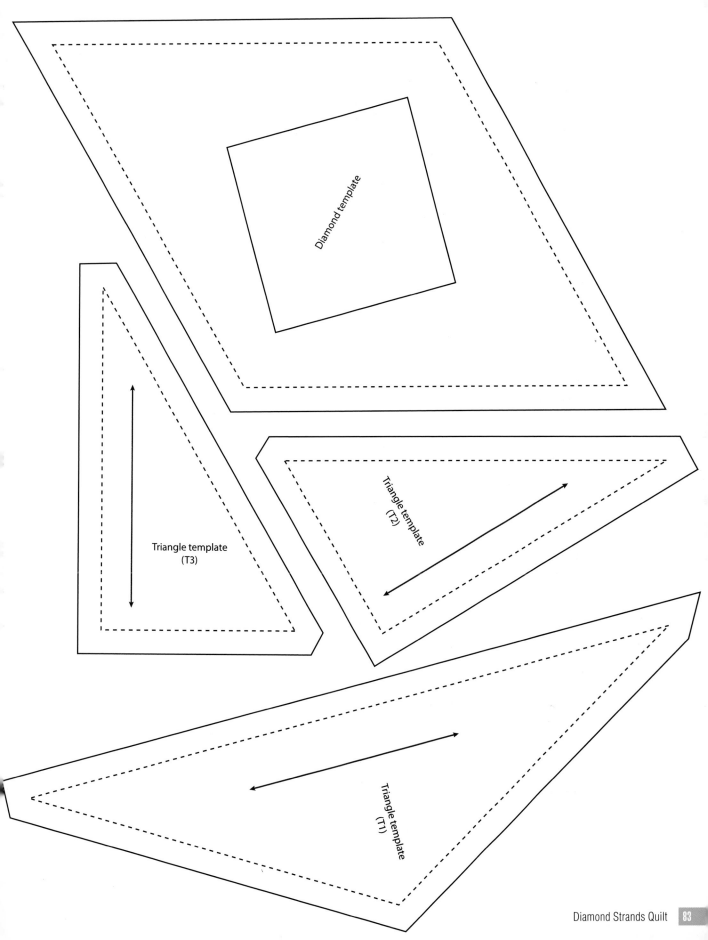

Diamond template

Triangle template
(T3)

Triangle template
(T2)

Triangle template
(T1)

## Materials

**4 prints:** scraps at least 6½˝ × 7˝ each (for exterior panels)

**Solid 1:** ¼ yard (for bottom, tabs, and optional strap)

**Solid 2:** ⅜ yard (for lining)

**Mid-/heavyweight sew-in interfacing:** ½ yard

**Lightweight fusible interfacing:** ¼ yard

**Single-sided fusible Peltex:** ⅛ yard (a very stiff stabilizer, fusible on 1 side)

**Zipper:** 12˝ or longer

**2 rectangular 1˝ metal rings** (optional for strap)

**Erasable fabric marker or chalk**

## Cutting

**FROM EACH PRINTED FABRIC:**

Cut 1 rectangle 6½˝ × 7˝

From Solid 1:

Cut 1 rectangle 8˝ × 5¼˝

Cut 2 rectangles 3½˝ × 4˝

Cut 1 rectangle 3½˝ × 15½˝ (optional for strap)

**FROM SOLID 2:**

Cut 2 rectangles 9˝ × 12˝

On each 9˝ × 12˝ rectangle cut out 2 squares 2¼˝ × 2¼˝ on each bottom (12˝) corner, to create the lining pieces (see Figure 1, page 86)

# essentials bag

**FINISHED BAG:** approximately 7˝ wide × 5½˝ tall × 4˝ deep

This is an adorable little bag with several functions. It can be a small purse, perfect for your wallet, phone, and a few essentials. Or without the strap, it can be a cute pouch just right for your toiletries when traveling. It features four print fabrics, with only small accents of solids on the strap and bottom.

**FROM THE MID-/HEAVYWEIGHT INTERFACING:**

Cut 4 rectangles 6½˝ × 7˝

From the lightweight fusible interfacing:

Cut 1 rectangle 8˝ × 3⅝˝

Cut 1 rectangle 3½˝ × 15½˝ (optional for strap)

**FROM THE FUSIBLE PELTEX:**

Cut 1 rectangle 8˝ × 4˝

# Construction

*All seams are ½" unless stated otherwise.*

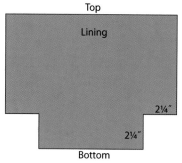

Figure 1

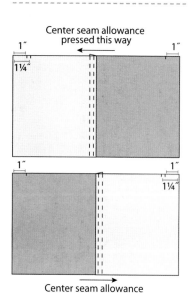

Figure 2

## Prepare the bag exterior panels

**1.** Pin a mid-/heavyweight interfacing rectangle (6 ½" × 7") to the wrong side of each print body rectangle of the same size. Baste with ¼" seams around all 4 edges.

Pin well before basting the interfacing, because as you sew the fabric will stretch but the interfacing will not.

**2.** Align and pin 2 body pieces, right sides together, and then sew together along a 7" side with a ½" seam. Press the seam to the left. Topstitch ⅛" or less from the seam along the pressed-under seam allowance, and then again ¼" from that. Repeat with the other 2 body pieces, pressing the seam to the right (Figure 2).

# Install the zipper

**1.** Mark 1″ from each end along the top raw edge of each exterior panel, right side up (Figure 2). Then mark 1¼″ from the end on the side that the seam allowance is pressed toward (left end on 1 panel, right end on the other).

> If the top of the zipper tape extends more than ¾″ beyond the top metal stops, trim it down ¾″ and, using a lit match, lightly burn the edge to prevent unraveling.

**2.** Align the top metal zipper stop with the 1¼″ mark on 1 exterior panel. Pin the zipper ¼″ from the top edge with the zipper pull facing down (Figure 3).

**3.** Use a zipper foot to stitch along the zipper ½″ from the top edge, starting and stopping 1″ from each end. Stitch close to the zipper but not right against it (Figure 3).

> Whenever you stitch along a zipper, it's best to start with the zipper halfway open. Start sewing until you get close to the zipper pull. Stop with the needle down in the fabric. Then slide the zipper pull open (or closed) to where you've already sewn, so it is out of your way, and finish sewing along the zipper. This prevents the little "bump" in your seam that you can sometimes get when going around the zipper pull!

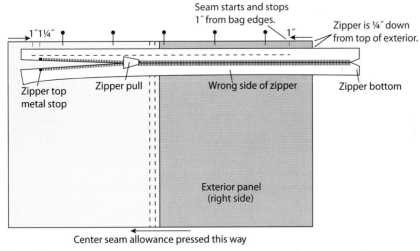

Seam starts and stops 1″ from bag edges.

Zipper is ¼″ down from top of exterior.

1″ 1¼″

1″

Zipper top metal stop

Zipper pull

Wrong side of zipper

Zipper bottom

Exterior panel (right side)

Center seam allowance pressed this way

Figure 3

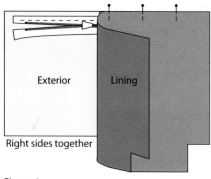

Right sides together

Figure 4

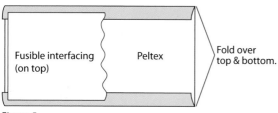

Fusible interfacing (on top)

Peltex

Fold over top & bottom.

Figure 5

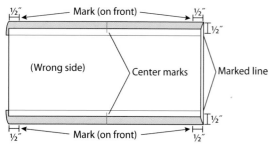

½″  Mark (on front)  ½″

½″

(Wrong side)

Center marks

Marked line

½″

½″  Mark (on front)  ½″

Figure 6

**4.** Pin a Solid 2 lining piece to the exterior panel, right sides together, as shown in Figure 4, aligning the top and side raw edges. Using a zipper foot, and placing the exterior side up (to see the previous stitching), sew through all layers just inside (zipper side) the previous seam, starting and stopping 1″ from each end (Figure 4).

**5.** Press both the exterior and the lining away from the zipper teeth. Pin in place and topstitch ⅛″ from the seam, starting and stopping 1″ from each end.

**6.** Repeat Steps 2–5 for the other side.

**7.** Sew a few wide zigzag stitches in place across the bottom of the zipper, ½″ inside the edge of the bag. Trim the zipper just beyond the stitches and burn the edge with a match. The stitches will keep the zipper from opening during construction.

## Prepare and install the bottom panel

**1.** Center the fusible side of the Peltex on the wrong side of the 8″ × 5¼″ Solid 1 rectangle. Fuse in place, following the manufacturer's instructions. Fold the long edges of the solid fabric to the back and iron in place. Center the 8″ × 3⅝″ rectangle of fusible interfacing on the back (Peltex side), fusible side down, and—making sure the folded-under fabric edges are underneath and stay wrapped tightly around the Peltex—fuse in place to hold it all together (Figure 5).

**2.** Use erasable fabric marker or chalk to mark ½″ from both ends on the front (fabric side) of each long edge. On the wrong (interfacing) side, mark the center of each long edge and draw a line parallel to and ½″ from each long edge (Figure 6).

**3.** Overlap 1 exterior panel ½″ along the marked line on the bottom panel, wrong sides of both pieces facing up, while also aligning the marked center of the bottom with the center seam on the exterior (Figure 7). Pin in place, making sure the lining is free and out of the way. Flip so that the right sides are up. Sew close to the edge of the bottom panel, starting and stopping at the ½″ marks and backstitching at both ends. From the back, clip the seam allowances at the ends of the seam (½″ mark).

**4.** Repeat Step 3 to pin together the other side of the bottom to the other exterior panel. Before flipping the piece, open the zipper all the way. Then flip it over to sew as instructed in Step 3.

**5.** Pull the zipper to ¾ of the way open.

## Complete the bag body and lining

**1.** Keep the bag inside out and pin back the lining so that it's out of the way at the top near the zipper. Pin the exterior panels together along one side, lining up the top and bottom (you will need to unfold the top). Making sure the lining and zipper stay free, sew a ½″ seam along one side edge. Trim the seam allowance to a narrow ¼″ near the zipper to help reduce the bulk (Figure 8). Unpin the lining and press the seam allowance open. Repeat for the other side.

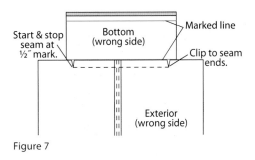

Start & stop seam at ½″ mark.
Bottom (wrong side)
Marked line
Clip to seam ends.
Exterior (wrong side)

Figure 7

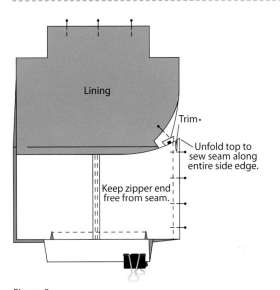

Lining

Trim.
Unfold top to sew seam along entire side edge.
Keep zipper end free from seam.

Figure 8

**tip**

Because the Peltex bottom is so stiff, it won't want to fold easily as you sew. Use a binding clip to keep it folded and out of your way as you sew.

**tip**

To press the side seam open, lay the seam flat on top of the bottom panel and use the tip of your iron. A tailor's ham, or even a rolled-up towel, inserted into the bag is helpful.

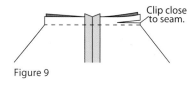

Figure 9

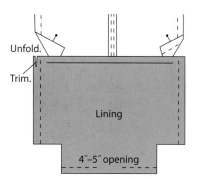

Figure 10

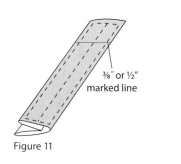

Figure 11

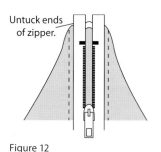

Figure 12

**2.** Flatten out one side so the bottom edge lines up with the short edge of the bottom panel (right sides together). Sew across with a ½″ seam, backstitching at each end. Trim close to the seam (Figure 9). Repeat for the other side.

**3.** Pin the 2 lining pieces together, right sides together, along each side and bottom, keeping the zipper and exterior panels out of the way and unfolding the top of the sides near the zipper. Sew the sides and bottom with a ½″ seam, leaving a 4″–5″ opening in the center of the bottom for turning (Figure 10). Trim the seam allowance to ¼″ near the zipper. Press the seams open using the tip of your iron.

**4.** "Pinch," sew with a ¼″ seam, and trim each bottom corner to create a boxed corner (page 119).

**5.** Turn the bag right side out through the opening in the lining; then tuck the lining into the bag.

# Make and attach the tabs

Whether or not you add a strap, you will need to make and attach tabs at both ends of the zipper. If you will be adding a strap, be sure to loop the tabs through the metal rings before sewing them on.

**1.** Press under ½″ on each short edge of a 3½″ × 4″ Solid 1 rectangle. Press in half along the long edge (4″). Open and press each raw edge in to meet at the center fold. Fold back along the center and press. Topstitch ⅛″ from the edge along all 4 sides and sew down the center (Figure 11). Repeat for the second tab.

**2.** Using chalk or a disappearing fabric marker, mark a line ⅜″ (½″ for the strapless version) from one short end on each tab (Figure 11).

**3.** Reach inside the lining opening to make sure the side seam allowances are open, especially up in the corners near the zipper. Untuck the ends of the zipper so they're not caught between the lining and exterior (Figure 12).

**4.** Close the zipper to 2″ from the top. Pinch that end of the bag into a flat point with the zipper on top (Figure 12), making sure the zipper teeth are close together and the lining is caught in the corner between your fingers. Everything needs to lie as flat as possible so you don't have to sew through too much bulk.

**5.** Fold the tab in half and, if adding a strap, loop it through a ring.

**6.** Place the tab centered around the pinched point (Figure 13) so that the marked line is just above the metal zipper stops. Make sure both ends of the tab are even on the front and the back and centered over the point, so that the seam will go across each end the same. When the tab is placed under the presser foot, it has a tendency to get crooked, so double-check before you start sewing.

Stitch on marked line placed just above metal stops.

Figure 13

**7.** Sew back and forth across the marked line 3 or 4 times (Figure 13). Go slowly; there's many layers of fabric. Your machine might get stuck, and you may have to turn it by hand to move the needle in and out of the fabric; but if you go slowly and carefully, you should be fine.

**8.** Now open the zipper to 2″ from the bottom. Pull the bottom end of the zipper out through the opening at that end. Poke your finger in the corner to flatten the seams and smooth things out so that there are no bunches in the fabric. Make sure the lining is up in the corner.

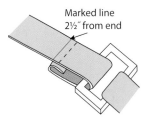

Marked line 2½″ from end

Figure 14

**9.** Pinch the end flat like the other side. Repeat Steps 5–7 for this side. There is no metal zipper stop to line up on this end, so line up the tab to overlap the point the same amount as the other side.

**10.** Hand stitch the opening in the lining closed.

# Make and attach the strap

The strap is optional. This process is essentially the same as for the tabs.

**1.** Iron the 15½″-long fusible interfacing strip to the wrong side of the 15½″-long Solid 1 strip. Fold the strip in half lengthwise and press. Open the strip and press each raw edge in to meet at the center fold. Fold back along the center and press. Topstitch ⅛″ in around all four edges and sew down the center.

**2.** Mark a line 2½″ from both short ends. Fold under ⅜″ on each end of the strap and press. Loop the folded ends through the outside of the rings and up to the marked lines. Sew across the straps close to the folded ends, forming a loop around each ring (Figure 14).

*And your bag is complete!*

# Steal the Show

Piecing solids as the focus of your project

## Materials

*Materials list is for all 3 panels.*

**Print 1:** ⅝ yard (green floral)

**Print 2:** ¼ yard (light blue floral)

**Print 3:** ¼ yard (medium blue floral)

**Print 4:** ¼ yard (dark purple print)

**Solid 1:** 1⅝ yards (medium purple)

**Solid 2:** ½ yard (light blue)

**Solid 3:** ⅛ yard (light green)

**Solid 4:** ⅜ yard (navy)

**6 canvas stretchers:** 15″ long
(available at art supply stores or online)

**6 canvas stretchers:** 30″ long

**Staple gun and ⅝″ staples**

**Erasable fabric marker**

## Cutting

*To avoid having to measure and remeasure several times, label each set of strips with the letter shown so you know exactly which to choose as you assemble the panels.*

**FROM PRINT 1:**
Cut 4 strips 1¼″ × width of fabric [A]

Cut 1 strip 7¼″ × width of fabric [B]

**FROM PRINT 2:**
Cut 4 strips 1⅜″ × width of fabric [C]

**FROM PRINT 3:**
Cut 2 strips 1½″ × width of fabric [D]

Cut 1 strip 1¾″ × width of fabric; crosscut into 3 strips 1¾″ × 13½″ [E]

**FROM PRINT 4:**
Cut 2 strips 2½″ × width of fabric [F]

# arts and crafts triptych

**3 UNFINISHED PANELS:** each 18½″ × 34″

**3 FINISHED ART PIECES:** each 15″ × 30″

Made in the classic Arts and Crafts (or Mission) style, this design of pieced solid fabrics enhanced with soft prints really shines. Together, the three panels, which are inspired by the stained-glass windows of that era, create a dramatic statement on your walls. They're pieced like regular quilt tops but mounted on canvas stretchers to hang as finished artwork.

**FROM SOLID 1:**
Cut 4 strips 4″ × width of fabric [G]

Cut 2 strips 1½″ × width of fabric; crosscut into 4 strips 1½″ × 13½″ [H]

Cut 2 strips 3″ × width of fabric [I]

Cut 2 strips 4¾″ × width of fabric; leave 1 strip uncut [J]; and crosscut 1 strip into 3 rectangles 4¾″ × 8¼″ [K]

Cut 4 strips 4¼″ × width of fabric [L]

*Cutting continued on page 96*

## FROM SOLID 2:

Cut 6 strips ⅞″ × width of fabric [M]

Cut 6 strips 1⅜″ × width of fabric [N]

## FROM SOLID 3:

Cut 3 strips 1″ × width of fabric; leave
2 strips uncut [O]; crosscut 1 strip
into 6 rectangles 1″ × 5⅞″ [P]

## FROM SOLID 4:

Cut 6 strips ⅞″ × width of fabric [Q]

Cut 6 strips 1″ × width of fabric; leave 1 strip
uncut [R]; crosscut 5 strips into 9 strips each
1″ × 18½″ for 3 [S] strips and 6 [T] strips

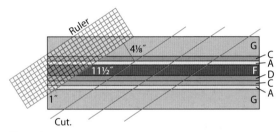

Figure 1

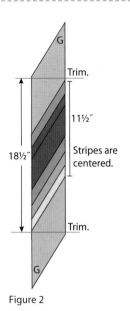

Figure 2

# Construction

*All seams are scant ¼″ unless otherwise noted.*

# Make Section 5

This section features the bold chevron designs.

**1.** Make 2 strip sets, placing solid and print strips
in the following order: G, C, A, F, D, C, A, G. Sew
the strips right sides together along the long
edges with a scant ¼″ seam allowance (Figure 1).
Press seam allowances in one direction.

**2.** Cut 1 set of strips diagonally to create half of
the chevron rectangles as shown in Figure 1: Cut
the diagonal strips by first lining up the ruler at
an angle so that the ruler measures 11½″ across
the print strips from outside edge [C] to outside edge [A] At the same time, make sure the
cutting line is at least 1″ from the side edge of
the strip set where it crosses the print [A] strip.
Make a cut all the way across the strip set at
this angle. Now, using the diagonal edge as a
guide, cut a strip 4⅛″ wide on the same angle.
Repeat twice to make a total of 3 strips.

### NOTE

Each time you cut, check that the angle creates
an 11½″ line across the print fabrics (Figure 2).
If it gets off, trim the start of the new chevron
before cutting to size. You might have enough
fabric to cut an extra chevron. If so, cut it so
you can use the most accurate strips.

**3.** Turn the strips vertically and trim the tops
and bottoms perpendicular to the sides to make
rectangles measuring 4⅛″ × 18½″. Make sure
to center the angled print fabrics so that there
is the same amount of solid fabric [G] at the
top and bottom of each rectangle (Figure 2).

**4.** Repeat Step 2 to cut the other half of the chevrons from the remaining strip set, this time cutting the angle in the opposite direction as shown in Figure 3. Trim the top and bottom ends as described in Step 3.

**5.** Sew 1 left and 1 right chevron together, with a 1˝ × 18½˝ Solid 4 strip [S] between the 2 chevrons as shown in Figure 4. Pin frequently, because the bias edges of these pieces may stretch. Press the seam allowances toward the center strip [S] Repeat to make a total of 3 Section 5 chevron units.

# Make Section 1

**1.** Make 1 strip set of Print 3 [E] and Solid 1 [H] strips, sewing along the long (13½˝) edges as follows: H, E, H, E, H, E, H. Press seam allowances toward the print fabrics.

**2.** Crosscut the H/E strip set, across the length, into 3 segments each 3½˝ × 8¼˝. Set aside (Figure 5).

**3.** Sew a long Solid 4 strip [R] along the top of a Print 1 strip [B] Press seam allowance toward the Solid 4 [R]

**4.** Crosscut the R/B strip, across the length, into 3 segments each 8¼˝ × 7¾˝ (Figure 5). There will be some leftover fabric, so you can choose the sections of the print you like best and fussy cut a bit.

**5.** Sew an H/E segment from Step 2 onto an R/B segment from Step 4 as shown in Figure 5. Press seam allowance toward Solid 4 [R] Repeat to make a total of 3 Section 1 units. Set aside.

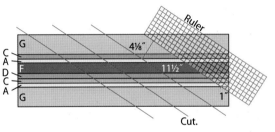

Figure 3

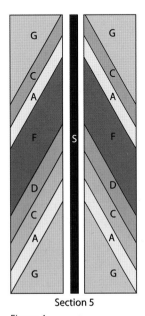

Section 5

Figure 4

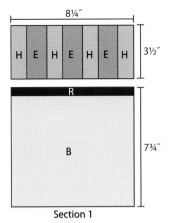

Section 1

Figure 5

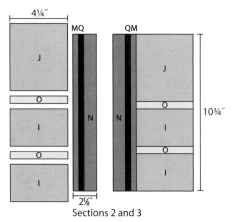

4¼″

MQ   QM

J

O

N   N

I

O

I

10¾″

2⅛″

Sections 2 and 3

Figure 6

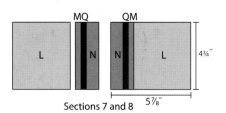

MQ   QM

L   N   N   L

4¾″

Sections 7 and 8   5⅞″

Figure 7

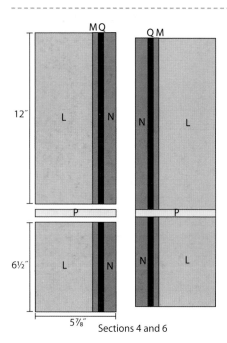

MQ   Q M

12″

L   N   N   L

P   P

6½″

L   N   N   L

5⅞″   Sections 4 and 6

Figure 8

# Make Sections 2 and 3

**1.** Make 1 strip set of Solid 1 [I and J] and Solid 3 [O] strips, sewing along the long edges as follows: J, O, I, O, I (Figure 6). Press seam allowances toward the Solid 1 fabric.

**2.** Crosscut this strip set, across the length, into 6 segments each 4¼″ × 10¾″ (Figure 6). Set aside.

**3.** Make 2 strip sets of Solid 2 [M and N] and Solid 4 [Q] strips, sewing along the long edges as follows: M, Q, N. Press seam allowances toward the Solid 4 [Q] fabric (Figure 6).

**4.** Crosscut each of these strip sets, across the length, into 6 segments each 10¾″ × 2⅛″ (Figure 6).

**5.** Refer to Figure 6 to sew together the segments from Steps 2 and 4. Make 3 sets with the MQN segments sewn on the right (Section 2) and 3 sets with these segments on the left (Section 3). Press toward the Solid 2 narrow strips.

# Make Sections 4, 6, 7, and 8

**1.** Make 4 strip sets of Solid 1 [L], Solid 2 [M and N], and Solid 4 [Q] strips, sewing along the long edges as follows: L, M, Q, N. Press the [L/M] seam allowance toward Solid 2 [M], and the other seams toward Solid 4 [Q]

**2.** Crosscut these strip sets, across the length, as follows:

Cut 6 segments 12″ × 5⅞″

Cut 6 segments 6½″ × 5⅞″

Cut 6 segments 4¾″ × 5⅞″ for Sections 7 and 8 (Figure 7)

**3.** Refer to Figure 8 to sew each of the 12″ segments to a 6 ½″ segment with a Solid 3 [P] strip between them. Make 3 sets with the MQN segments sewn on the right (Section 4) and 3 sets with these segments on the left (Section 6). Press away from Solid 3 [P]

# Finish the construction

**1.** Use the assembly diagram at right as a guide to sew the sections into rows with a ¼″ seam. Use the 4¾″ × 8¼″ Solid 1 [K] rectangle for the center segment of the bottom row. Press the seam allowances toward the Solid 2 [N] strips.

**2.** Finish the panel by sewing the rows together with a Solid 4 [T] strip between each. Press the seam allowances toward the Solid 4 [T] strips. Repeat Steps 1 and 2 to make 3 panels.

# Mount on canvas stretchers

**1.** Assemble the canvas stretcher frames according to the manufacturer's directions to make 3 frames 15″ × 30″. Make sure the corners are square; then staple to secure them in place.

**2.** Lay a frame on the right side of a panel, taking care to center it as accurately as possible on the design. Use an erasable fabric marker to trace the frame on the front of the panel. These will act as reference lines as you stretch the panel onto the stretchers.

**3.** Flip the panel over, wrong side up, and lay the stretchers *face-down* (with the sloped side down) and centered on it. Start in the middle of one side and fold the fabric around to the back of the stretchers, stretching it slightly and stapling in place. The reference line should wrap about ¼″ around the side of the bar.

**4.** Apply a staple at the middle of the opposite side bar, using the reference line to stretch the panel the same amount as the other side. Move to the two unsecured sides and, in the same manner, staple the middle of each one.

**5.** Switch back and forth between the two pairs of sides, slowly stapling either side of the middles and working toward each of the corners. Place staples about every 1″. Take care to stretch the panel uniformly so that it does not have ripples or become distorted. The reference lines should be straight along the side of the stretcher bars.

**6.** Tuck in the excess fabric at each corner to create a neat triangular fold on the top or bottom edge. Use several staples to secure the folded corner on the back. Trim any excess fabric when stapling is complete.

**7.** Repeat Steps 2–6 to complete the 3 panels.

*Now hang them up and enjoy your beautiful new artwork.*

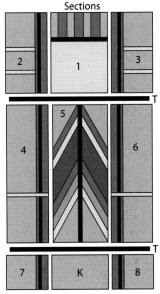

Sections

Assembly diagram

## NOTE

Because the chevrons are cut on the bias, they will stretch a great deal and distort the panel; you cannot stretch as much as you would for a regular canvas.

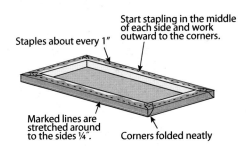

Start stapling in the middle of each side and work outward to the corners.

Staples about every 1″

Marked lines are stretched around to the sides ¼″.

Corners folded neatly

## Materials

**Linen/linen blend:** ⅝ yard for 14″ or 16″ pillow; ¾ yard for 18″ pillow (for front and back)

**Solid 1:** 1 fat quarter (for the vine)

**Solid scraps:** (for berries)

**Print scraps:** (for berries)

**Square pillow form:** 14″, 16″, or 18″*

**Steam-a-Seam 2 fusible web:** 1 sheet 9″ × 12″

*The cover is sewn ½″ smaller than the pillow form for a nice, firm pillow.*

## Cutting

**14″ PILLOW**

**From linen:**

Cut 1 square 14½″ × 14½″

Cut 1 rectangle 11″ × 14½″

Cut 1 rectangle 8½″ × 14½″

**16″ pillow**

**From linen:**

Cut 1 square 16½″ × 16½″

Cut 1 rectangle 13″ × 16½″

Cut 1 rectangle 8½″ × 16½″

**18″ pillow**

**From linen:**

Cut 1 square 18½″ × 18½″

Cut 1 rectangle 15″ × 18½″

Cut 1 rectangle 8½″ × 18½″

**For all sizes**

**From Solid 1:**

Cut 1 bias strip 1″ wide across the diagonal of the fabric.

# berry vine pillow

**FINISHED SIZE:** 13½″ square, 15½″ square, or 17½″ square

Beautiful textured linen makes a nice backdrop for some fun, modern circles (the "berries"). The raw-edge appliqué makes this pillow a cinch to complete. I made it with a combination of prints and solids, but it would work equally well with all solid fabrics. Instructions and yardage are provided for three different sizes—14″, 16″, and 18″ pillow forms.

# Construction

*All seams are ½″ unless otherwise noted.*

## Prepare the appliqués

*Templates are on page 103.*

**1.** Trace the templates onto the Steam-a-Seam 2 to make 7 each of the 2″- and 1¼″-diameter circles, and 6 each of the 1¾″- and 1″-diameter circles. If preferred, use fewer appliqués on the smaller pillow or more on the larger one.

**2.** Cut loosely a little outside each circle. Peel off the unmarked side of the paper and stick it onto the wrong side of the solid and print scraps. Now cut precisely on the lines through all layers.

## Sew the vine

**1.** Fold both long edges of the bias strip in ¼″ to meet in the center; press.

A bias tape maker is a nifty little tool that will make the pressing of the bias strip a snap. You just feed in your strip and it comes out the other side folded so you can press it. No more burned fingers! For this project you'd need a ½″ bias tape maker. Of course, you can also buy premade fusible bias tape, but where's the fun in that?

**2.** Lay your bias tape wrong side down onto the right side of the linen square (14½″, 16½″, or 18½″). Arrange the bias tape into a squiggle or any shape desired. The bottom end should extend off the edge of the square. Pin it in place with plenty of pins. To get the bias tape to lie flat, stretch the outside edge as you go around a curve. Cut the top end to the desired length, tuck it under ¼″, press, and pin.

**3.** Topstitch close to the edge along all sides of the bias tape, keeping the tape flat as you sew.

## Add the berries

**1.** Pair the circles, placing a 1¼″ circle on top of each 2″ circle and a 1″ circle on top of each 1¾″ circle. Peel the backing paper off the smaller circles and stick them in place on the larger circles so that they are off-center.

**2.** Peel the paper off the larger circles and stick them along the vine in a somewhat random manner. Use the photo (page 103) as a guide if you desire. Add extra circles or remove some if desired. When you are pleased with the arrangement, fuse them in place according to the manufacturer's instructions.

**3.** Topstitch close to the edge all the way around each circle.

# Complete the pillow

**1.** Hem (page 119) each remaining linen rectangle by pressing under ½″ along one long edge. Tuck the raw edges into the fold and press again. Topstitch ⅛″ from the folded edge.

**2.** Lay the smaller hemmed rectangles on top of the larger one, right sides facing up, overlapping the hems to create a square the same size as the front (14½″, 16½″, or 18½″). Pin in place and baste along the sides ¼″ from the edges (Figure 1).

**3.** Pin the pillow front and back together, right sides together. Stitch around all 4 sides with a ½″ seam. Trim corners and turn right side out through the back opening.

**4.** Insert the pillow form through the opening in the back.

*Now find a spot where your new pillow can be admired.*

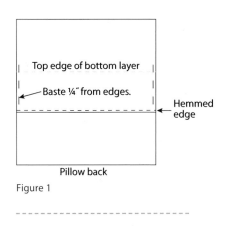

Top edge of bottom layer

Baste ¼″ from edges.

Hemmed edge

Pillow back

Figure 1

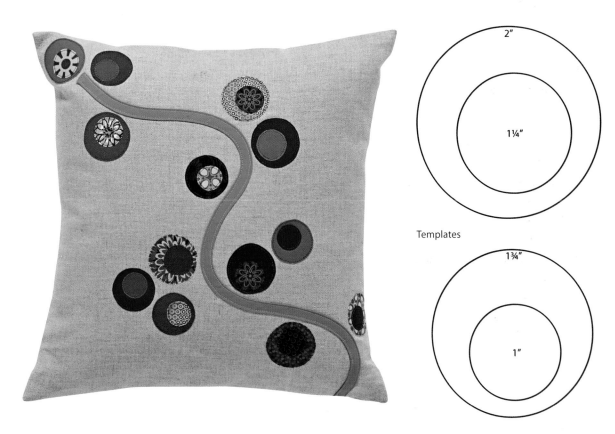

Templates

# pretty pinwheels quilt

FINISHED SQUARE: 10″ × 10″

FINISHED QUILT: 40¼″ × 40¼″

## Materials

**Print 1:** ⅓ yard (for pinwheels)

**Print 2:** ½ yard (for pinwheels and Border 2)

**Solid 1:** ½ yard (for square backgrounds)*

**Solid 2:** 1⅛ yard (for square backgrounds and Border 3)

**Solid 3:** 1½ yards (for outlines, sashing, Border 1, and back accent strip)

**Backing:** 1⅜ yards (plus Solid 3 backing strip)

**Binding:** ⅜ yard for straight-grain binding (⅝ yard for bias binding)

**Batting:** 48″ × 48″ piece (or packaged crib size)

### NOTE
Print 1 and Solid 1 should be of similar tone and color. The same goes for Print 2 and Solid 2.

Sweet and simple is in order for a new baby girl. These pinwheels highlight darling prints with coordinating solids, and their straight lines keep them modern and clean. The piecing might look complicated, but strip piecing and cutting down to size later saves a lot of time and energy. For your two blocks to look like opposites, you need to choose two prints, each with a matching solid.

## Cutting

**FROM PRINT 1:**

Cut 4 strips 2″ × width of fabric

**FROM PRINT 2:**

Cut 4 strips 2″ × width of fabric

Cut 4 strips 1¼″ × width of fabric (for Border 2)

**FROM SOLID 1:**

Cut 1 strip 8⅞″ × width of fabric; crosscut into 4 squares 8⅞″ × 8⅞″, and cut each square twice diagonally into 4 quarter-square triangles (16 total)

**FROM SOLID 2:**

Cut 2 strips 8⅞″ × width of fabric; crosscut into 5 squares 8⅞″ × 8⅞″, and cut each square diagonally twice into 4 quarter-square triangles (20 total)

Cut 4 strips 3″ × width of fabric (for Border 3)

**FROM SOLID 3:**

Cut 20 strips ⅞″ × width of fabric; leave 16 strips uncut. Crosscut 2 strips into 6 rectangles ⅞″ × 10½″, and crosscut 2 strips into 2 strips ⅞″ × 31¼″

Cut 4 strips 1¾″ × width of fabric (for Border 1)

Save the remaining fabric for backing strip.

### tip

Starching Solids 1 and 2 before cutting will make sewing the triangles easier with less stretching on the bias edges. Be sure to wash your entire quilt after it is complete to protect it from insects that are attracted to starch.

## Construction

*All seams are a scant ¼″ unless otherwise noted.*

## Sew the pinwheel strips

**1.** Sew a ⅞″ uncut Solid 3 strip to each long side of a 2″ Print 1 and a 2″ Print 2 strips to make 8 strip sets. Press the seam allowances toward the Solid 3.

**2.** Crosscut the strip sets, across the length, into 8″ × 2¾″ segments. Cut 20 segments of Print 1 and 16 of Print 2.

## Construct the blocks

**1.** Sew a Solid 2 triangle to each Print 1 segment as shown in Figure 1. Overhang the triangle ⅛″ (or less) at the top of the strip to allow for trimming later. Press the seam allowances toward the Solid 3 strip. In the same manner, sew a Solid 1 triangle onto each Print 2 segment.

**2.** Align a ruler with the top edge of the Print 1 segment, then square up the corners at a right-angle (Figure 2), trimming off the overhang from the previous step (see Note).

> ## NOTE
>
> The overhang is added in case your piece doesn't come out square and you need a little extra fabric to compensate. When squaring up the corner, align the ruler edge along the edge of the 8″ pieced segment and trim along the triangle overhang (Figure 2). Do not trim the long edge of the pieced segment, because any change in width of this strip will be very obvious in the final product.

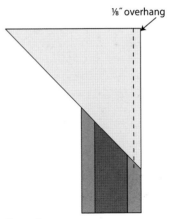

⅛″ overhang

Figure 1

**3.** Use the corner of the 8″ pieced segment and the 45° line on a rotary ruler to trim all the pieces down to triangles (Figure 2).

**4.** Refer to the block assembly diagram below to sew paired triangles together, pressing seams toward the Solid 3 strips. Then, sew the triangular block halves together. Press the seam open or see Tip for an alternative pressing method.

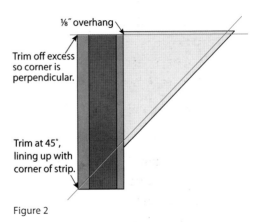

⅛″ overhang

Trim off excess so corner is perpendicular.

Trim at 45°, lining up with corner of strip.

Figure 2

To enhance the pinwheel effect, I wanted to make the Solid 3 strips stand out on my quilt. To do this I did some nontraditional pressing when I pieced the blocks. I pressed toward the Solid 3 strip along the Solid 2 triangle. Then, on the same seam, I switched to pressing the seam open along the pieced print segment, and finally, switched back to pressing along the Solid 3 strip at the next Solid 2 triangle. It may seem fussy, but this pressing process really added a nice touch to my finished quilt.

**5.** Trim the blocks to 10½″ × 10½″, making sure to trim all sides equally to keep the piecing centered.

Block assembly diagram

# Complete the quilt

**1.** Use the quilt assembly diagram below as a guide to sew the 3 blocks into 3 rows with a ⅞″ × 10½″ Solid 3 sashing strip between each block. Then, sew the rows together with a long ⅞″ × 31¼″ sashing strip between each row. Pin the sashing before sewing and press the seam allowances toward the sashing.

In this project, it's important that the sashing is cut to length (not just sewn on before cutting). This will help keep your blocks from stretching on their bias edges. Pin the sashing to the blocks before sewing to prevent stretching.

**2.** Refer to Quiltmaking Basics (pages 119-124) to piece and sew on the 3 borders and to layer, baste, quilt, and bind your quilt. Be sure to take measurements and pin carefully when adding borders, because the bias edges of the squares could stretch. Use the remaining Solid 3 to piece an accent strip for the backing.

*If your baby girl can't yet sleep with a blanket, she can enjoy this quilt on the floor.*

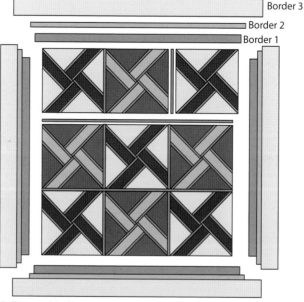

Border 3

Border 2

Border 1

Quilt assembly diagram

## Materials

**Solid 1:** ⅔ yard (for pocket)

**Solid 2:** ½ yard (for backing)

**Print fabric 1:** ¼ yard (for binding)

**Medium-weight sew-in interfacing:** ⅓ yard

**Extra-firm, heavyweight sew-in stabilizer:** ¾ yard
(Timtex, available from C&T Publishing, or Peltex)

**Mat board or pressed cardboard:** 7½″ × 12″ and
13¼″ × 12″ pieces (available at craft supply stores)

**⁷⁄₁₆″ metal eyelets, or grommets and
installation tool**

## Cutting

**FROM SOLID 1:**

Cut 1 rectangle 13¼″ × 9″

Cut 1 rectangle 19¼″ × 10″ (for pocket exterior)

Cut 1 rectangle 19¼″ × 9¾″ (for lining)

*Label the pocket exterior and lining pieces to aid
in assembly. The lining is cut slightly smaller so it
will fit neatly inside the pocket when assembled.*

**FROM SOLID 2:**

Cut 1 rectangle 14¼″ × 13″

Cut 1 strip 6″ × 15″

Cut 1 strip 2″ × 15″

Cut 2 strips 9″ × 2″

# wall pocket

**FINISHED SIZE:** 14¼″ width × 13″ height × 3″ depth

This nifty pocket is so handy for storing file folders or magazines in your craft room—or even bedtime books in a child's bedroom. Made mostly of solid fabric, it has a simple, modern look that can be made to match any color scheme. It's got a stiff backing and grommet holes for your hooks.

**FROM PRINT 1:**

Cut 2 strips 2¼″ × width of fabric.

**FROM INTERFACING:**

Cut 1 rectangle 19¼″ × 10″

**FROM HEAVYWEIGHT STABILIZER:**

Cut 1 rectangle 12¼″ × 9⅜″

Cut 1 rectangle 14¼″ × 13″

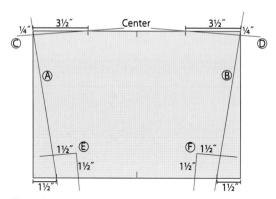

¼″  3½″        Center        3½″  ¼″
Ⓒ                                    Ⓓ

Ⓐ                              Ⓑ

1½″ Ⓔ            Ⓕ 1½″
    1½″        1½″

1½″                        1½″

Figure 1

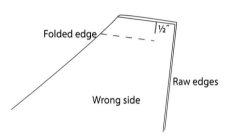

Folded edge                ½″

                        Raw edges
        Wrong side

Figure 2

# Construction

All seams are ½″ unless otherwise stated.

# Make the pocket and lining

**1.** Refer to Figure 1 to mark the pocket exterior (19¼″ × 10″) and lining (19¼″ × 9¾″). Mark 3½″ in from each top corner and 1½″ in from each bottom corner. Mark the center of the top and bottom edges.

**2.** Refer to Figure 1 to cut the contour shape of the pocket exterior and lining pieces. Cut lines [A] and [B] from each 1½″ bottom mark to its corresponding top corner. Make cuts [C] and [D] from the 3½″ top marks to ¼″ down from the top corner. Finally, cut out 1½″ squares at the bottom corners [E and F]; they won't be perfectly square, but that's okay.

**3.** Lay the pocket exterior on top of the interfacing rectangle and pin well around the edges. Baste ⅛″ from all edges. Trim the interfacing to match the pocket piece.

**4.** Fold the bottom corner of the pocket exterior, with fabric right sides together and the 1½″ edges lined up (Figure 2). Mark ½″ from the raw edge. Sew from the marked line to the folded edge with a ½″ seam, backstitching at both ends. Repeat for the other corner and both corners of the lining piece. Turn the corners of the pocket exterior right side out.

**5.** Position the lining inside the pocket exterior, wrong sides together. Line up all edges and pin together along the sides and bottom. Make sure the corner seams line up and the seam allowances are open, creating a ½″ slit at each corner (where the seams end). Baste ¼″ from the edge on the 3 sides.

**6.** Draw a line that is 1⅜″ down and parallel to a long edge of the 12¼″ × 9⅜″ stabilizer rectangle. Fold on this line and press. Mark the center of the other long edge (top).

**7.** Insert the pressed stabilizer rectangle (from Step 5) between the 2 pocket layers so that the pressed edge sits at the same angle as the corners, as shown in Figure 3. Also insert the 12″ × 7″ mat board between the lining and the stabilizer. Line up the top center marks of the exterior, lining, and stabilizer and pin along the top edge. Baste ⅛″ from the top edge, keeping the mat board away from the stitching.

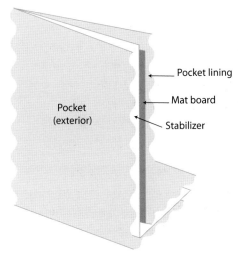

Figure 3

# Prepare and apply the binding

*Refer to Double-Fold Straight-Grain Binding (pages 121-124) for specifics on making and sewing the binding.*

**1.** Prepare double-fold binding from the Print 1 strips.

**2.** Sew the binding to the top edge of the prepared pocket.

Stitching the binding to the back by hand will be very difficult in this case because of the stiffness of the pocket. Instead use the stitch in-the-ditch machine method described in Quiltmaking Basics (pages 124).

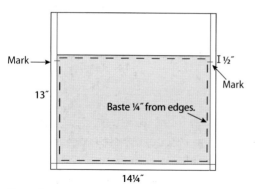

Mark →

13″

I ½″

← Mark

Baste ¼″ from edges.

14¼″

Figure 4

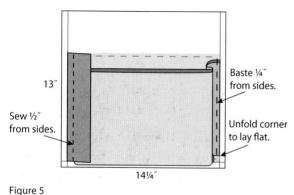

13″

Sew ½″
from sides.

Baste ¼″
from sides.

Unfold corner
to lay flat.

14¼″

Figure 5

14¼″

Figure 6

# Attach the pocket to the base

**1.** Draw lines on the 14¼″ × 13″ stabilizer rect-angle ½″ from the sides and bottom edge (14¼″). Mark the center of the bottom edge.

**2.** Lay the 13¼″ × 9″ Solid 1 rectangle, right side up, on the stabilizer so the sides and bottom edges line up with the drawn lines. Baste ¼″ from the edge on all 4 sides. Make a mark ½″ down from each top corner of the Solid 1 rectangle (Figure 4).

**3.** Lay the pocket, right side up, on top of the basted Solid 1 base rectangle, lining up the top of the pocket sides with the ½″ top marks. Align and pin the side raw edges of the pocket with the sides of the base rectangle, opening the unstitched part of the bottom corners to keep the raw edges even. Baste ¼″ from the edges on the two sides (Figure 5).

## tip

The stiffness of the stabilizer and cardboard can make sewing around the pocket dif-ficult. Take your time, and do your best to keep the raw edges even and straight.

**4.** Lay a 2″ × 9″ Solid 2 strip along one side of the basted pocket, right sides together. Line up the raw edges and the top and bottom with the base rectangle (Figure 5). Pin in place and stitch with a ½″ seam. Open the strip out over the stabilizer and press flat. (It will hang over the edge of the stabilizer, and that's okay; trim it later.) Repeat for the other side.

**5.** Line up the bottom of the pocket with the base rectangle, aligning the raw edges and center marks. Baste ¼″ from the bottom pocket edge (Figure 6). Again, the corners can be tricky, but open them up to keep the raw edges even.

**6.** Lay the 15″ × 2″ Solid 2 strip along the bottom of the basted pocket, right sides together, aligning the raw edges and letting the strip hang off both sides of the stabilizer. Pin in place and stitch with a ½″ seam (Figure 7). Open out over the stabilizer and press flat.

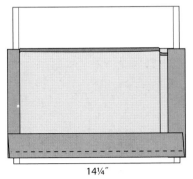

14¼″

Figure 7

**7.** Lay the 15″ × 6″ Solid 2 strip along the top edge of the base rectangle, right sides together, aligning the raw edges and letting the strip hang off both sides of the stabilizer. Pin in place, keeping the pocket itself free, and stitch with a ½″ seam. The stitches will just miss the sides of the pocket. Open the strip out over the stabilizer and press flat.

**8.** Flip over and trim all sides of the fabric even with the stabilizer base.

## Finish the pocket

**1.** Align the 14¼″ × 13″ Solid 2 rectangle, right side up, onto the back of the stabilizer. Pin in place and baste ⅛″ from the edges through all layers along the sides and bottom only.

**2.** Insert the 13¼″ × 12″ mat board rectangle into the top opening between the stabilizer and back fabric. Baste ⅛″ from the top edge.

**3.** Apply the remaining prepared binding to the edges of the base, just as you would to finish a quilt (pages 123-124). Machine stitch it to secure the back. Move the mat board slightly as you sew so that it will not get caught in the seams.

**4.** Mark 1⅜″ in and down from each top corner. This will be the center of the eyelet holes. Follow the manufacturer's directions to apply the eyelets.

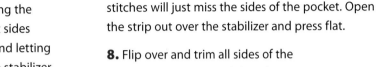

You will have to cut holes through all layers. The fabric and stabilizer can be cut with scissors, but you'll need to use a craft knife to cut the mat board. Work slowly, cutting small arc sections of the circle several times until you get through the whole thickness, and then move on to the next section.

*Hang two hooks on the wall 11½″ apart, and you're ready to organize!*

# the basics

Practical
information and
tips for sewing
and quiltmaking

I'm a pretty relaxed sewist. Before anything professional ever came out of my sewing, this is what I did for fun. So I don't like to stress too much about things like perfect points. I'm fairly accurate because I'm surprisingly patient when needed, but you won't find me doing any unnecessary steps. I also do almost everything by machine if possible, because hand sewing just isn't my strength.

If you have no experience in sewing or quilting, you should probably get yourself a good book on the basics or take a beginner class or two. But I did want to include some of the essentials here, just in case you need a refresher as you go along. I have my own way of doing things, which isn't necessarily the "right" way, but you can try my methods and figure out what works best for you.

# Techniques

## Cutting

A rotary cutter, rotary ruler, and a cutting mat are a must for the projects in this book. I recommend that you use a cutting mat at least 18″ × 24″ and a clear plastic rotary ruler (6″ × 24″). Square, clear plastic cutting rulers in various sizes (especially 12″ or larger) are also useful.

To become an accurate cutter, the single most important thing you can do is to take your time. And because those blades are quite sharp and dangerous, it's doubly important.

If fabric amounts are tight and the pieces need to be laid out a specific way, you'll find a cutting diagram with the projects in this book. If not, it's best to cut in the order listed—often the largest pieces first.

Many of the projects call for cutting strips across the width of the fabric. Here's how to do this accurately: Fold your fabric in half so the two selvages meet. If you haven't prewashed and the fold from the bolt is still there, you can use that as long as it's flat. If not, don't expect the cuts in the store to be straight. That means don't worry about the top and bottom ends of the selvages lining up.

What's important is that the fabric lies flat when it is folded so the selvage edges are parallel.

Now, take the fold and line it up with a line on your cutting mat. Next, trim off one raw edge of the fabric so that it is perpendicular to the fold. This is called squaring up the fabric. This is a crucial step, so that when you open your strips they are straight across the fold and don't have a little dip because they were cut at an angle.

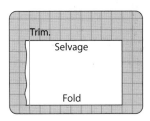

Now you can cut an even strip by lining up your ruler with the square edge of the fabric that you just cut. If you will be cutting a lot of strips, it's a good idea to check your edge about every four to six strips to make sure it is still perpendicular. Trim it again if necessary.

## Pinning

I'm not a pinner. As I mentioned, I'm pretty laid back about sewing (this is supposed to be fun, right?). So unless I think I really need them, I avoid pins. Some obvious exceptions to this would be when I need points to match perfectly, to hold some fabric out the way of my seams, if I'm doing my borders correctly, or if I'm using interfacing (which doesn't stretch like fabric).

Throughout the book I may or may not instruct you to pin. So, if I suggest pinning, it is usually for a good reason. On those projects where I don't suggest pinning, if you feel more comfortable pinning and want to do more precise work, then by all means, pin away.

## Pressing

In general, press seams toward the darker fabric to avoid the seam allowance showing through the lighter fabric. For some projects, I provide specific directions on which way to press the seams. In these projects, the pressing direction is important to the assembly process. Press lightly in an up-and-down motion; pressing in a back-and-forth motion could distort the shape. Avoid using a very hot iron or overironing, which can also distort shapes and blocks. Be especially careful when pressing bias edges because they stretch easily.

## Seams

I use either a ½″ or ¼″ seam for the projects in this book. For each project, I have noted the seam allowance at the beginning of the construction. Pay close attention and sew the seams accurately, because sewing accurate seams is the key to successful piecing. When sewing a ¼″ seam, actually using a scant ¼″ seam will help you be even more accurate. A scant ¼″ seam is simply sewn with the needle positioned a thread width less than ¼″.

It's a good idea to do a test seam before you begin sewing. Cut three strips of scrap fabric 2″ × 5″ each, and sew them together on the long edges with a scant ¼″ seam. Press the seams to one side, and you should have a 5″ × 5″ square. When testing a ½″ seam, the finished size should be 4″ × 5″. If you don't get the right size, repeat the test, altering your seam allowance as needed until you are accurate.

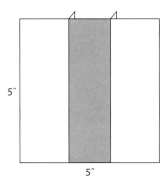

Here are additional tips for sewing seams:

If a seamline will be crossed by another seam that will anchor it, there is no need to backstitch at the ends.

When two previous seams meet a new seam, if the seam allowances are pressed in opposite directions, this will allow the seams to nest and thus naturally line up.

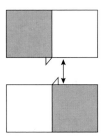

## Hems

A hem is used to finish an edge of fabric so that it won't rip or fray. I use double-fold ¼" hems for projects in this book. To do this, press under ½" along the raw edge of the fabric. Tuck the raw edges into the fold and press again. Topstitch ⅛" from the folded edge.

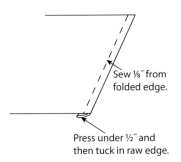

Sew ⅛" from folded edge.

Press under ½" and then tuck in raw edge.

## Boxed Corners

Most of the three-dimensional projects, such as the Gradations Bag (page 39) and Quilted Camera Case (page 71), have flat sides or bottoms. These are created by sewing boxed corners. It's a lot easier than it looks. Here's how:

First, squares are cut from the corners before the pieces are sewn together. The accuracy of the position of the cut-out squares isn't so important. As long as both squares are cut the same size, the boxed corners will look fine. Next, the side and bottom seams are sewn together to join the front and back pieces of the project.

Finally, with the project turned inside out, "pinch" each bottom corner, right sides together, so that the side seam and bottom seam line up and the raw edges create a straight line. Stitch across the raw edges with a ¼" seam, back-stitching at both ends. Trim close to the seams.

Clip close to seam.

When the project is turned right side out, the pinched and sewn corners will be flat with boxed sides.

## Quiltmaking Basics

These pointers are geared specifically to the quilt projects in this book, but you'll find that some of them apply to other sewing projects as well.

## Chain Piecing

This technique saves a lot of time (and thread) when you are piecing together many identical pairs of pieces. After you sew the first pair, don't lift the presser foot and cut the thread. Instead, continue sewing right off the edge of one set and then just feed the next pair in under the lowered presser foot.

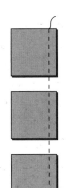

Try to do all of the same pairs of pieces right in a row. When you're done, you'll have a long string of connected pairs; simply clip the threads between them and press. Repeat this process for each new piece you add onto the blocks.

## Borders

When border strips are cut on the cross-wise grain, piece the strips together to achieve the needed lengths. It's best to piece with a diagonal seam (see Binding, page 122) to make the seam less noticeable.

## SQUARED BORDERS

All the quilts in this book use squared borders—no mitered corners here!

In most cases the side borders are sewn on first. When you have finished the quilt top, take three vertical measurements—one through the center and one at each side. Take the average of these three measurements (if they are different), and this will be the length to cut the side borders.

Place pins at the centers of all four sides of the quilt top, as well as in the center of each side border strip. Pin the side borders to the quilt top first, matching the center pins and then the edges. Using a ¼″ seam allowance, sew the borders to the quilt top and press toward the border.

Next, measure horizontally across the center of the quilt top and at the top and bottom, including the side borders. Average these three measurements, and this will be the length to cut the top and bottom borders. Repeat, pinning, sewing, and pressing.

# Backing

Plan on making the backing a minimum of 6″–8″ longer and wider than the quilt top. Piece, if necessary. Trim the selvages before you piece to the desired size. To economize, piece the back from any leftover quilting fabrics or blocks in your collection.

Although you may find that you're tired by the time you get to backing your quilt, it's a great place to get creative. When using leftover fabric from the project, I like to add some design elements that hint at the design on the front of the quilt. For example, if my quilt top is all squares and stripes, I might include a stripe or two across the back and add an off-center square.

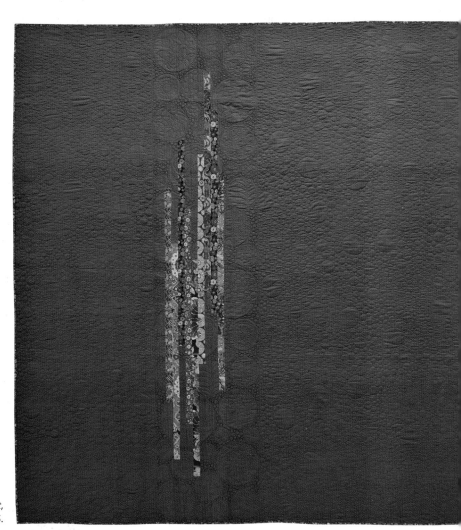

Backing of *Pebble Road Quilt*, page 15.

## Layering

Start by cutting the batting down to approximately 8″ longer and wider than your quilt top.

Spread the backing, wrong side up, on a clean, flat surface and tape the edges down with masking tape. (If you are working on carpet, you can use T-pins to secure the backing to the carpet.) Center the batting on top, smoothing out any folds. Place the quilt top, right side up, on top of the batting and backing, making sure it is centered.

## Basting

Basting keeps the quilt "sandwich" layers from shifting while you are quilting.

If you plan to machine quilt, pin baste the quilt layers together with safety pins placed 3″–4″ apart. Begin basting in the center and move toward the edges first in vertical, then horizontal, rows. Try not to pin directly on the intended quilting lines.

I find that spray basting before pinning helps to keep everything nice and flat. Be sure to spray in a well-ventilated area and cover the surface around the quilt with newspaper to protect from overspray. After layering, peel back sections of the batting and quilt top and spray the backing. Smooth the top layers back in place. Repeat until you've covered the whole backing. Now do the same process but peel back only the quilt top. This will secure the top to the batting. Then pin every 12″ for security.

If you plan to hand quilt, baste the layers together with thread using a long needle and light-colored thread. Knot one end of the thread. Using stitches approximately the length of the needle, begin in the center and move out toward the edges in vertical and horizontal rows approximately 4″ apart. Add 2 diagonal rows of basting.

## Quilting

Quilting, whether by hand or by machine, enhances the pieced or appliquéd design of the quilt. You may choose to quilt "in-the-ditch," echo the pieced or appliqué motifs, use patterns from quilting design books and stencils, or do your own free-motion quilting. The designs you choose for quilting will impact the look of your finished quilt. You can use it to highlight some elements, add movement, or even just blend into the background. Sometimes quilters add motifs in their quilting that echo the subject matter of the quilt top. Whatever you choose, be sure to consider wisely and not just make it an afterthought. And, remember to check your batting manufacturer's recommendations for how close the quilting lines must be.

It should also be noted that many gorgeous quilts (including those in this book) have been quilted by a professional on a long-arm machine (see Quilting Services, page 127). This is an added expense, but you might find that the results are worth it. In many cases I quilt my own quilts for control of design and cost-saving reasons, but I do find it's sometimes difficult (and very time-consuming) to get the results I want on my own sewing machine. If you work with a quilter, you will be able to have input into the design, but they will also offer you expert advice.

## Binding

After the quilting is completed, trim the excess batting and backing from the quilt even with the edges of the quilt top.

To calculate the length of binding you need, add the dimensions of all 4 sides and add an extra 10″ (15″ for bias binding). For example if your quilt is 30″ × 50″, then you calculate 30 + 30 + 50 + 50 + 10 = 170″.

## DOUBLE-FOLD STRAIGHT-GRAIN BINDING

If you want a ¼″ finished binding, cut the binding strips 2″ wide (or 2¼″ if you will sew down the back by machine as I do). To determine how many strips you need, divide the total length of the binding by 40″ (width of fabric). In the example above you need 170″ / 40″ = 4.25; rounding up that's 5 strips.

Piece the strips together with diagonal seams to make a continuous binding strip. Trim the seam allowance to ¼″. Press the seams open.

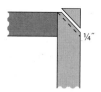

Press the entire strip in half lengthwise with wrong sides together. See Attaching the Binding (page 123) for directions and tips on sewing the binding to your quilt.

## CONTINUOUS BIAS BINDING

Continuous bias binding involves using a square sliced in half diagonally and then sewing the resulting triangles together. You then mark strips, sew again to make a tube, and cut to make a continuous binding strip of the desired length. The same instructions can be used to cut bias for piping.

Again, if you want a ¼″ finished binding, cut the binding strips 2″ wide (or 2¼″ if you will sew down the back by machine as I do).

To determine the size of the square you need, first find its area by multiplying the length of binding you need by the width of the binding strips. Our example would be 170″ × 2.25″ = 382.5. Take the square root of that number to get the size square needed. The example would be a 20″ square.

If you want to avoid doing the math, just take the yardage requirement provided and cut the largest square you can. For example, if yardage is ½ yard, you cut an 18″ × 18″ square.

Now, cut the square in half diagonally, creating two triangles.

Sew these triangles with right sides together as shown, using a ¼″ seam allowance. Press the seam open.

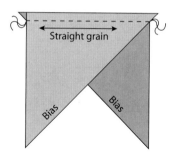

Using a ruler, mark the parallelogram created by the 2 triangles with lines spaced the width you need for your bias binding (2″ or 2¼″). Cut about 5″ along the first line.

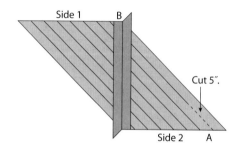

Join Side 1 and Side 2 to form a tube. The raw edge at line A will align with the raw edge at B. This will allow the first line to be offset by one strip width. Pin the raw edges right sides together, making sure that the lines match. Sew with a ¼″ seam allowance. Press the seam open. Cut along the drawn lines, creating one continuous strip.

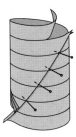

Press the entire strip in half lengthwise with wrong sides together. See Attaching the Binding (below) for directions and tips on sewing the binding to your quilt.

### ATTACHING THE BINDING

Open one short end of the binding and fold it diagonally with wrong sides together as shown. Press. Then trim the excess fabric, leaving about ¼″ beyond the fold. Refold the binding lengthwise.

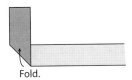

Fold.

Trim.

## NOTE

This trimming on the diagonal is for the tuck-in method of finishing binding that I use. If you use a different method to finish the ends of your binding, this might not be necessary.

With raw edges even, pin the binding to the front edge of the quilt a few inches away from the corner, leaving the first few inches of the top side of the binding unattached.

Open the binding strip and start sewing the bottom layer with a backstitch, using a ¼″ seam allowance. Sew the binding onto the quilt for about 4″, stitching only through the bottom layer of the binding. Then, remove the needle and cut the thread. Fold the top layer back down and start sewing at the point you left off, through all layers.

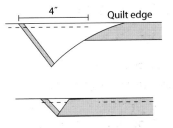

4″     Quilt edge

Stop sewing ¼″ away from the first corner and backstitch one stitch. Lift the presser foot and needle. Rotate the quilt one-quarter turn.

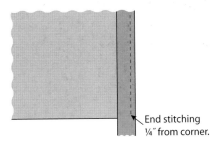

End stitching ¼″ from corner.

Fold the binding at a right angle so it extends straight above the quilt and the fold forms a 45° angle in the corner.

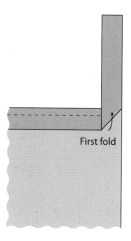

First fold

Then bring the binding strip down even with the edge of the quilt.

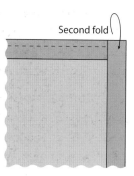

Second fold

Begin stitching again at the top of the new edge, backstitching at the start. Repeat at each corner.

Continue stitching until you are back near the beginning of the binding strip. Leave the needle down and trim away the excess tail, leaving it long enough to tuck into the opening left at the start. Tuck the tail into the fold of the starting end that was left unsewn, making sure the raw edges are even. Continue sewing through all layers until past the start of the first seam.

Hand stitch or machine stitch the angled fold of the outside layer to the tucked-in tail to keep it secure.

Trim the edges of your batting and quilt layers even with the raw edge of your binding (¼″ wide).

Fold the binding over the raw edges to the quilt back and either hand stitch or machine stitch it in place. Overlap the binding at the corners to make a mitered fold.

I prefer to machine stitch the binding to the back. To do so, use binding clips to hold the folded-over binding securely around to the back. On the backside, the folded binding edge should cover the stitches that attach it. Flip to the front side of the quilt and stitch in-the-ditch along the binding seam, removing binding clips as you come to them. It's important to stop and check the back every once in a while, because if you're not careful to keep the binding folded all the way around, your stitching can miss the folded edge and you will have to go back and fix it. Some people find this method frustrating, but as I mentioned before, I'll do anything I can to avoid hand stitching. Once you practice a bit, you'll find it goes rather quickly.

## Labels

All good quilts deserve a label. Think of it as an artist's signature. It can really be anything from your name embroidered on the back, to a label full of information, such as:

Who pieced the quilt

Who quilted the quilt

The date

The location

The title

Who it was made for (and date of birth for a baby)

A message to the recipient

You can write the information with a fabric marker, print it with your computer, or even embroider it by hand or machine. Usually it's on a small separate piece of fabric, hand stitched in place after the quilt is complete.

I like to add a little decoration, like some piecing similar to the quilt top. Since it's just a label, I keep it small and don't worry about it being a little rougher. You can use muslin, or better yet, some of the lovely solids from the quilt.

I'm not that consistent with how I label my quilts, but I do like to include my name and the date at the very least. I also "sign" my quilts with my maiden-name initials satin-stitched into the bottom right corner. I do this through all layers after the quilt is complete.

A label ensures that everyone, for many years to come, will remember who lovingly made the quilt.

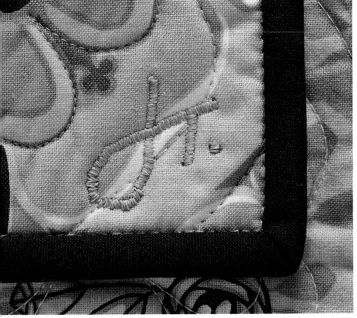

# About the Author

Jessica Levitt has been sewing and quilting since the age of 12. Always thirsting for some new craft, she has taught herself countless quilting techniques as well as costuming, event design, and home decor. She has also designed several lines of fabric for Windham Fabrics. Her degree in engineering from Duke University is now largely unused while she pursues fulfillment in these more creative endeavors. Jessica lives and works in New Jersey with her husband and two children. You can see her latest projects and catch up on her life at her blog: www.juicy-bits.typepad.com.

# Resources

Buy quality quilter's cotton at your local quilting store or online at the many wonderful fabric websites. The fabrics used in this book come from many different designers, manufacturers, and retailers. Designs are changed frequently, so check the manufacturers' websites to see their current collections.

Some manufacturers whose fabrics are used in this book include the following:

Art Gallery Fabrics
www.artgalleryquilts.com

Free Spirit Fabrics
www.freespiritfabric.com

Henry Glass & Co.
www.henryglassfabrics.com

Michael Miller Fabrics
www.michaelmillerfabrics.com

Moda Fabrics
www.unitednotions.com

Riley Blake Designs
www.rileyblakedesigns.com

The *Traffic Jam* Quilt features their collection "Wheels."

Robert Kaufman Fabrics
www.robertkaufman.com

All the solids used in this book were Kona Cottons provided by Robert Kaufman. For colors by project, see Solid Colors by Project (page 127).

Westminster Fabrics
www.westminsterfabrics.com

Windham Fabrics
www.windhamfabrics.com

Timber—my first collection as a designer—is distributed by Windham.

## Other Resources

### The Warm Company

www.warmcompany.com

My favorite kinds of batting are Warm & Natural and Warm & White, by The Warm Company, who provided all the batting for the quilts in this book.

I also use their fusible web Steam-a-Seam 2.

## Quilting Services

All the quilts in this book were quilted by—

Angela Walters

www.quiltingismytherapy.com

## Solid Colors by Project

This is a list of the Robert Kaufman Kona Cotton Solids used in each project. A color card with all the colors available can be purchased from the company website.

*Pebble Road* Quilt: Charcoal, Coal

Linen Apron: Sable

*Frame Up* Quilt: White

*Color Block* Tablecloth: Amber, Raisin

*Gradations* Bag: Navy, Dusty Blue

*Traffic Jam* Quilt: Peridot, Amber, Caribbean, Robin Egg, Rich Red, Curry, Chocolate, Snow

*Stripe of Strips* Pillow: (Version 1) Teal Blue (main pillow), Caribbean, Cyan, Glacier, Bayou; (Version 2) Sage, Aloe, Robin Egg, Aqua

*Boyfriend* Quilt: Tan, Cream, Bone, Champagne, Ivory, Eggshell, Snow, Raffia, Khaki, Straw

*Twin String* Quilts: Midnight, Dusty Blue, Cerise

Quilted Camera Case: Rich Red

*Diamond Strands* Quilt: Chocolate, Olive

*Essentials* Bag: (Version 1) Black, (Version 2) Seafoam

*Arts and Crafts Triptych*: Dusty Blue, Artichoke, Lupine, Indigo

*Berry Vine* Pillow: Grass Green (stem), Avocado, Crocus, Bright Periwinkle, Hibiscus, Magenta, Purple

*Pretty Pinwheels* Quilt: Sage, Petal, Cactus

*Wall Pocket*: Cactus, Olive